THE TYRANT
Modern Slavery
Can You See It?
A Book by Justin Boynton

Table of Contents

The Tyrant
Modern Slavery
Can You See It?
Copyright © 2025 by **Justin M. Boynton**

This is a work of nonfiction. Every effort has been made to ensure accuracy; however, the author and publisher assume no responsibility for errors, omissions, or the interpretation of the material presented. This book is not intended as legal, medical, or psychological advice. Readers should consult qualified professionals where appropriate.

Published by Justin M. Boynton
ISBN: 979-8-9892234-9-7
For information, contact:
voiceoftheforgottenusa@gmail.com

INTRODUCTION: WHO IS YOUR MASTER?

Who is the tyrant in your life? Does it have a face, does it have a name? Does it look at you or does it influence you?

There is an oppressive presence that fills the Earth, enslaving all of mankind. But this presence has a trick up its sleeve: deceit. The deceit blinds you from seeing the truth, and from seeing your enslavement. I will show you in this book concrete evidence of your very own enslavement. Don't ignore this, don't look away, don't put your head in the ground and ignore this warning.

The truth is heavy, yes. The truth is almost unbearable. Almost. For those who wish to see the truth, I will show it. I do not write to you in vain. I write with the sole purpose of opening your eyes to the truth. It would be much easier to write books about "The 7 Habits of Highly Successful People," "Passive Income Secrets," and "Intermittent Fasting for Beginners." But I'm not here to sell books. I'm here to rip the veil off of your eyes so that those who want to see can see.

Everything (and I mean absolutely everything) within your being will tell you not to read this! Close the book and run away. "This is a lie," the whisper says. But this is the time that we live in. The time that was spoken about within God's guide for our lives. They will see lies as the truth and the truth as lies. What is bitter will taste sweet, and what is sweet will be bitter.

"What sorrow for those who say that evil is good and good is evil, that dark is light and light is dark, that bitter is sweet and sweet is bitter." (Isaiah 5:20, NLT)

1

I know what I'm about to share with you will expose the darkness, the lies, and the deceit so openly that you may not finish the book because of the weight of the truth.

Everything in your life, without exception, was changed from its original design to enslave you. Anything built by man, who is contaminated, contains the ingredient of enslavement.

If man builds something, they build it with the knowledge and understanding that is within their minds. The mind cannot build anything unlike itself. Just as an apple tree cannot produce oranges, a human mind cannot produce uncontaminated thought.

Your house enslaves you. You are a slave to your car. Your government enslaves you. Even the smallest items, like your cellular phone, enslave you. Forces not seen of this world enslave you, but they will become visible once they are revealed to you.

You cannot live anywhere on this world that is habitable without a government enslaving you. Nowhere on this earth can you live freely. This is the level of bondage that we have around us. And you're not even aware of it!

Government speaks of freedom while they enslave you. This is an incredible deceit that even the politicians themselves believe in.

"America is free," you will hear. There is nothing free about America, and there is nothing free about this world. Governments are contaminated by darkness (greed, selfishness, hate) and they enslave you to produce for them.

How many people work to produce income for the government so that the government can live off the backs of others? And this is just the tip of the iceberg. What I'm going to show you is not only what you can see with your eyes and understand with your mind, but I'm going to show you the source of all of this enslavement.

Jesus talked about us being slaves and us being blind, but it's almost impossible to understand it with deceit guiding our minds. I will show you what is hidden, and then you can decide if you want to choose the darkness that enslaves or the light that sets you free.

You might think the tyrant is your boss, your government, or the corporations. And in a sense, you'd be right. But they are merely puppets. The real tyrant, the one pulling all the strings, has a name you probably weren't expecting. But before I tell you his name, you need to see his work.

Follow me on this journey, this adventure to a new level of consciousness that will make you uncomfortable, but can also set you free.

Here is the path we will walk together:

First, I will show you the prison you cannot see, through one man's story that is every man's story.

Then, I will show you who profits from your enslavement, the web of greed that takes from your life with every transaction.

Next, I will show you the laws that force your compliance, the invisible chains you obey without questioning.

Then, I will reveal the spiritual force behind it all, the one who contaminates this system.

Finally, I will show you what freedom requires.

But before we begin, you must understand something about the man you're about to meet.

John is more than one man. John embodies everyman. You are John. His numbers are real, drawn from actual costs in Columbus, Ohio.

Billions of people experience the same struggles he does. His story is a mirror. When you see John, you are seeing yourself.

The truth is here. What you're about to see cannot be unseen.

Let's go.

PART ONE: JOHN'S STORY

MONDAY: THE ALARM

Let's start the story out in Columbus, Ohio.

John lives in a residential area in North Columbus, surrounded by homes that all look pretty similar. At 6 o'clock on Monday morning, his alarm goes off. He checks his phone for any messages that came in overnight before getting out of bed and getting ready for the workday. The first thing he sees? Three emails from his boss that came in at 11 PM last night. His boss doesn't sleep. Or rather, his boss expects John not to sleep either. The emails can wait; he's not paid for the time between 11 PM and 6 AM. But the anxiety they create? That's free. That comes with the job.

He presses start on the coffeemaker, a $300 machine he bought because the office coffee is terrible and stopping at Starbucks every day was costing him $150 a month. He's being "financially responsible." The machine will pay for itself in two months, he told himself. What he didn't calculate was the cost of the premium beans, the filters, the descaling solution, and the eventual repairs. Or the fact that the machine was designed to break after the warranty expires. Built to fail. Another hand in John's pocket.

He throws some breakfast in the microwave and eats it while watching the time on his cell phone. The breakfast burrito cost $3.50 at the grocery store. It costs $0.70 to make. But John doesn't have time to make breakfast. He's already behind. He's always behind.

At 6:30 AM, he grabs the key fob to his car and goes out and starts it. The car (a 2019 Honda Accord he bought used with 35,000 miles on it because he's "responsible") cost him $24,000. He put $4,000 down (his entire tax return that year) and financed the remaining $20,000 at 6.5% interest. Over five years, he'll pay $27,840 for this $24,000 car. The bank makes $3,840 for doing nothing except creating money on a computer and calling it a "loan."

But wait, it gets better. That $24,000 sticker price? The car dealer paid $19,900 for it at auction. That's a $4,100 profit margin. So, the car that cost $19,900 will ultimately cost John $27,840. That's a 40% markup on the actual cost.

And that's before insurance. Before gas. Before maintenance. Before registration fees. Before the inevitable repairs that will be needed; the original owner did not sell a 2019 Accord with 35,000 miles, because everything was perfect on the car.

It takes him 27 minutes on average to get to work, and he checks drive time on Google Maps to make sure he'll arrive on time. Google Maps, free service, right? Wrong. Google is tracking his every movement, building a profile of his behavior, selling that data to advertisers, insurance companies, anyone who will pay. John's commute data is worth money. Google is making money off John's enslavement. Even his "free time" has been monetized.

John sees there's a backup on I-71, and he begins to stress over arriving on time. Now Google says he's going to arrive at work at 7:04 AM.

His boss is very strict and insists everyone should be there five minutes early before they start work. Not on time. Early. Work starts at 7 AM, but if you arrive at 7 AM, you're late. John is salaried, which means he's expected to work 40 hours per week. But that's the lie. He actually works 50+ hours and gets paid for 40. The extra 5-10 hours? Free labor for the company. They don't call it slavery. They call it "being a team player."

THE TYRANT

John knows his boss is going to give him a lecture upon arriving. His boss will criticize him for not being responsible and making sure he gets up in time. Never mind that John woke up at 6 AM. Never mind that the traffic was beyond his control. Never mind that arriving at 7:04 means John will stay until 4:10 out of guilt to "make up the time" even though he's salaried and the time shouldn't matter. None of that matters.

What matters is the fear. The fear keeps John compliant. The fear keeps John working those extra hours. The fear keeps John checking his email when he's not on the clock.

He arrives at the workplace, just as Google Maps predicted, and John's boss lectures him for three minutes about responsibility, about punctuality, about setting a good example for the team. The lecture costs John nothing monetarily. But it cost him his dignity. It cost him his peace. It cost him the first hour of his workday because now he's rattled, anxious, unable to focus.

This is the invisible cost of enslavement. The cost that never appears on a spreadsheet.

John works. He processes reports. He attends meetings. He responds to emails. He does work that generates approximately $400 per day in value for the company. The company pays him $288 per day ($75,000 salary divided by 260 working days). The company keeps the remaining $112.

That's called profit. The company calls it "return on investment." The truth calls it greed. John creates $400 of value. He receives $288. Someone else takes $112 for the privilege of "giving him a job."

Multiply that by 260 days per year. The company takes $29,120 from John's life annually. Over a 40-year career, that's $1,164,800 of John's life that goes to people who didn't create the value. They just owned the system that allowed the value to be created.

John finishes his workday at 4:00. Or rather, at 4:15 because he had to "make up" those four minutes from this morning. He doesn't even bother to check Google on his way home. He will arrive when he arrives. Google Maps cannot change the traffic.

But John doesn't realize that someone tracked his departure time. Someone tracked his route home. Google knows he stopped at the gas station, and because he tapped his phone to pay, Google knows he spent $14.99. Google knows he sat in his car for three minutes after parking in his driveway before going inside. Google knows everything. And Google sells everything.

John arrives home, parks his car, goes into his house, and gets a beer. A six-pack of craft IPA that cost him $14.99. He's not a heavy drinker. He just needs something to take the edge off. Something to help him transition from "work John" to "home John." The beer industry makes $15 billion per year off people like John, who just need to take the edge off.

He sits down just to relax before the responsibilities of home life kick in. But his mind is already running through the list:

-Mow the lawn (it's getting long; the HOA will send a violation notice)
-Pay the electricity bill (due tomorrow)
-Set aside time to talk to his wife, Sarah. Their eight-year-old daughter is 'having trouble focusing in class' according to Mrs. Henderson (another parent-teacher conference)
-Fix the leaking faucet in the bathroom (been putting it off for three weeks)
-Take out the trash (it's Monday; trash day is Tuesday morning)

None of these things are relaxation. All of these things are maintenance of the life he's enslaved to.

John will have to repeat this pattern approximately 240 times over the next year.

But this is just Monday. Let's see what the rest of John's week looks like.

TUESDAY: THE BREAKING POINT THAT NEVER COMES

Tuesday morning, John wakes up at 5:45 AM instead of 6 AM. He learned his lesson yesterday. Better to be early than to face his boss's lecture again. He checks his phone. Four new emails, two from his boss, sent at 1 AM.

His boss is always working. Or at least, always emailing. John wonders if his boss actually sleeps or if he just sets delayed-send emails to create the illusion of constant vigilance. Either way, the message is obvious: *You are never off the clock.*

Today, John skips breakfast. He'll grab something from the vending machine at work. This is not a good financial decision; that granola bar will cost $2.50 when he could have brought one from home for $0.75. But he doesn't have time. He's too tired. He's always too tired.

The commute is smoother today. He arrives at 6:52 AM, eight minutes early. His boss walks by his cubicle at 6:58 and grunts approval. No words. Just a grunt. This is what John has been reduced to: a worker who receives grunts of approval from another worker who has also been reduced to nothing.

At 10 AM, there's a mandatory all-staff meeting. "Mandatory" means if you don't attend, you're not a "team player." The meeting lasts 90 minutes. They could have sent an email. They could have summarized the entire meeting in three bullet points. But that's not how the tyrant works. The tyrant needs you in a room, watching a PowerPoint, listening to your boss talk about "synergy" and "paradigm shifts" and "thinking outside the box."

The real purpose of the meeting? To remind you that you are a slave. To remind you that you must obey. To remind you that you have no choice. The meeting is a power display. The company is the king. You are the servant. Bow.

During the meeting, John's phone buzzes. It's his wife, Sarah. The text says: "My car is making a weird noise. Can we take it to the shop this week?"

John's stomach drops. Sarah's car. The 2017 Toyota Camry they bought used three years ago. It's supposed to be reliable; it's a Toyota. But they're still paying $285 per month on it for another two years.

He texts back: "How bad?"

Sarah: "Sounds like grinding when I brake."

Brakes. Could be $300. Could be $1,000 if the rotors are damaged. John doesn't have $300. John definitely doesn't have $1,000.

He has $847 in his checking account. His next paycheck comes on Friday. It's $2,305 after taxes. One of the two he gets each month. And that money is already gone.

Monthly bills:

- Mortgage: $2,400 (he'll have to pull $95 from savings to cover the difference)
- Car payments: $674 (John's Honda $389 + Sarah's Toyota $285)
- Car insurance: $285 (both cars)
- Student loan: $380
- Utilities: $285
- Daycare: $1,200
- Groceries: $500
- Gas: $320

Total: $6,044.

John's two paychecks total $4,610.

THE TYRANT

Sarah works part-time as a dental hygienist, 30 hours a week at $28 an hour. She brings home about $2,800 a month after taxes.
But here's what that costs:

- Daycare so she can work: $1,200/month
- Her car payment: $285/month
- Her share of insurance: $105/month
- Her gas: $120/month
- Work clothes/supplies: $90/month

Total cost of Sarah working: $1,800/month.
Sarah's net contribution to the household: $1,000/month.
So, their real combined income is:
John: $4,610/month
Sarah (net): $1,000/month
Total: $5,610/month.

But the expenses don't stop at $6,044. John has been plugging the gap with credit cards for six months. He now owes $8,400 at 22.99% APR, with minimum payments of $240/month.
Add that to the bills, and they're at $6,284 every month.
Against $5,610 of income.
They are $674 short every month. And that hole only deepens.
The credit card companies love John. They get roughly $1,900 a year in interest from him. Over ten years, if he keeps scraping by on minimums, he'll pay close to $28,000 just to service an $8,400 balance. But John can't think about ten years. He can barely think about this week. And this week, Sarah's car needs repairs.

This is the tyrant's deceit: keep you so busy surviving that you never realize you're dying.

WEDNESDAY: THE ILLUSION OF PROGRESS

Wednesday morning. 5:45 AM. The alarm goes off. John has been asleep for six hours and forty-five minutes. He needs eight hours to function optimally. He's been running on a sleep deficit for seven years. The first thing he does is check his phone. Six emails. Two from his boss (sent at 5:30 AM, does this man ever sleep?). Four from various automated systems: his bank alerting him his balance is low, Amazon confirming a package delivery, his insurance company reminding him his car insurance renewal is coming up, and a promotional email from a credit card company offering him a "pre-approved" $15,000 credit line at "only" 24.99% APR.

The credit card email is not an accident. The tyrant knows John is drowning. The tyrant is offering John a lifeline that's actually a noose. John deletes the email. He's not that desperate. Not yet.

Coffee. Shower. The same rushed routine. Sarah is already up, getting the kids ready for school. Their daughter needs $20 for a field trip. Their son needs new shoes. He's growing fast, and his current pair is too small. Sarah asks if they can afford the shoes this week.

"How much?" John asks.

"Maybe $50 at Target?"

The mechanic called with the estimate: $650 for new brake pads and rotors. John does the math. The $650 for the car brakes is getting paid tomorrow. If he adds $50 for shoes, that's $700 on the credit card this week. That's manageable. Barely.

"Yeah, we can do that," John says. But what he means is: "We can go deeper into debt for that."

He grabs his keys and heads for the door. 6:25 AM. If he leaves now, he'll make it on time.

The commute is the same. I-71 eastbound, 35 minutes of stop-and-go traffic, NPR on the radio talking about inflation, about the cost of living, about how the economy is "strong" while John sits in his financed car, burning gas he can barely afford, heading to a job that underpays him.

He arrives at 6:55 AM. Safe. His boss walks by at 7:02 and doesn't even acknowledge him. Yesterday, John got a grunt of approval for being early. Today, he gets nothing for being on time. The goalpost for approval always moves.

At 9 AM, there's a surprise announcement. The company is implementing a "new productivity initiative." Translation: they're cutting staff and redistributing the work among remaining employees. John's department is losing two people. John's workload is increasing by approximately 25%. His pay is not increasing.

This is called "efficiency." It is the theft of a life. You are now doing the work of 1.25 people for the pay of one person. The company will save approximately $90,000 per year by firing two people and crushing the remaining staff.

Where does that $90,000 go? To the shareholders. To the executives. To the people who don't do the work but own the system that extracts "value" from the work.

John's boss pulls him aside after the announcement. "I know this is tough, but I'm counting on you to step up. You're one of my best people."

This is manipulation.

John is not one of the best people. John is one of the most compliant people. John is the one who won't quit when the workload becomes unbearable because John has a mortgage and a car payment and credit card debt and kids who need shoes.

John is trapped. His boss knows this. The company knows this. The tyrant knows this.

Fear is the tool of the tyrant. Fear of missing the mortgage payment. Fear of defaulting on credit cards. Fear of watching that three-digit credit score collapse and taking everything with it.

This is a system designed to enslave through fear, and fear keeps everyone in line.

"I'll do my best," John says. Because what else can he say?

The rest of the day is a blur of work. Emails. Reports. Deadlines that were already unrealistic and are now impossible. John skips lunch again. He drinks three cups of coffee. His heart rate is elevated. His stress level is through the roof. But he keeps going because stopping is not an option.

At 3 PM, he gets a calendar notification: "Performance Review Scheduled, Tomorrow 2 PM."

Performance reviews. The annual ritual where your boss tells you all the ways you've failed to meet expectations that were never clearly defined, then gives you a 2% raise that doesn't keep up with inflation, and tells you to "keep up the good work."

John has been with this company for four years. His starting salary was $68,000. His current salary is $75,000. That's a $7,000 increase over four years. That's an average annual raise of $1,750, or 2.6% per year.

Inflation over those same four years has averaged 4.2% per year. Which means John is making less money today than he was four years ago in real terms. His paycheck number went up, but his purchasing power went down.

The company calls this "competitive compensation." It is a gradual pay cut disguised as a raise. Deceit covers greed's tracks here.

John leaves work at 4:30 PM today, 30 minutes late because he's already behind on the projects that just became his responsibility.

On the drive home, he stops at the gas station. It cost $68 to fill the tank. He pays with his credit card because every dollar in his checking account matters right now.

The guy next to him at the station is charging a Tesla. No gas costs for that guy. Just electricity. John thinks about electric cars for a moment. They're better for the environment. They're cheaper to operate. They make sense.

But they cost $45,000 minimum. And John can barely afford the gas in his Honda.

This is the tyrant's trap: the solutions to your problems cost money you don't have. You stay trapped because escaping the trap requires resources that the trap prevents you from accumulating.

John gets home. Sarah's car is already parked in the driveway. She picked it up from the shop. $650 charged to the credit card. They fixed the brakes. It's good for now. Until something else breaks.

Dinner is leftovers from last night. Spaghetti, reheated in the microwave. The kids complain, but they eat. After dinner, John plays with his son for 20 minutes before homework time. His son wants to play catch in the backyard, but it's already dark. They play inside instead, tossing a foam football back and forth in the living room.

This is the only moment of joy in John's entire day. Twenty minutes of throwing a foam football with his eight-year-old son.

At 8 PM, John opens his laptop. He needs to prepare for tomorrow's performance review. This year, he needs to document his accomplishments, his value, and why he deserves more than a 2% raise. He types for an hour. Doing it makes him feel pathetic. He's begging for scraps from people who already take most of what he produces.

At 9:15 PM, his laptop battery dies. He forgot to plug it in after working for over an hour. He's too tired to go find the charger. After closing the laptop, he goes to bed.

Tomorrow is Thursday. Tomorrow is the performance review. Tomorrow is the day he has to smile and nod while his boss tells him he's "meeting expectations" and gives him a raise that's actually a pay cut.

This is Wednesday.

Only two more days until the weekend.

THURSDAY: THE PERFORMANCE REVIEW

Thursday morning. 5:45 AM. John wakes up exhausted. He's been dreading today since the calendar notification popped up yesterday afternoon.

Performance reviews are designed to make you feel grateful for whatever crumbs they throw at you. You walk into the meeting thinking about a raise, a promotion, recognition for your work. You walk out feeling lucky to still have a job.

This is psychological warfare. This is how the tyrant keeps you compliant.

John goes through his morning routine on autopilot. Coffee. Shower. Protein bar for breakfast because there's no time for anything else. He's running late because he couldn't sleep last night, his mind spinning with what he's going to say in the review, how he's going to advocate for himself, what percentage raise he should ask for.

He arrives at work at **6:58 AM**. His boss is already at his desk, door closed, on a phone call. John wonders if his boss lives at the office. Or if the office has become his boss's life and there's no distinction anymore.

The morning is consumed with the 25% additional workload that's now John's responsibility. The two people who were let go had projects in progress. Those projects don't disappear just because the people are gone. The work still exists. It just falls on whoever remains.

John is now managing four projects simultaneously. Before this week, he was managing two. His stress levels have doubled. His pay has not.

At 2 PM, his calendar alerts him: "Performance Review, Conference Room B."

John closes his laptop, grabs his notebook, where he's documented his accomplishments, and walks to the conference room. His boss is already there, sitting at the head of the table with a thin folder in front of him.

"Have a seat, John," his boss says.

John sits.

His boss opens the folder. Inside is a single sheet of paper: John's performance review form. The boss slides it across the table.

John looks at the ratings:

- Quality of Work: Meets Expectations
- Productivity: Meets Expectations
- Teamwork: Meets Expectations
- Communication: Meets Expectations
- Initiative: Meets Expectations

Everything is "Meets Expectations." Not "Exceeds." Not even in one category. Just a flat line of adequacy.

At the bottom, in the section labeled "Compensation Adjustment": 2.5%

John does the math really quick. 2.5% of $75,000 is $1,875 per year. That's $156 per month. After taxes, that's approximately $110 per month.

His car insurance just went up $15 per month. His electricity bill went up $25 per month. Groceries are more expensive by at least $50 per month compared to last year. Gas is up $40 per month.

That's $130 per month in increased costs.

His "raise" is $110.

He's losing $20 per month. His boss just told him "congratulations" for becoming poorer. The company calls this "competitive compensation." It's a pay cut with a smile.

Inflation ran 4.2% last year. John got 2.5%. That's a 1.7% pay cut disguised as a raise.

He's making less money this year than last year in real terms. And they expect him to be grateful.

"As you can see," his boss says, "you're doing solid work. Meeting all the key metrics. The company appreciates your contributions."

John looks at the paper. Four years of 50-hour workweeks. Four years of answering emails at midnight. Four years of missing his kids' bedtimes because he was working late. Four years of stress and anxiety and sacrificing his health.

Meets Expectations.

"I was hoping for something more than 2.5%," John says carefully. "Especially with the additional responsibilities I'm taking on with the staff reduction."

His boss nods, as if he expected this. "I understand. Unfortunately, this year's budget is tight. We're working with limited resources. But I want you to know that you're valued. This is the best I could do given the constraints."

This is the script. The boss delivers it every year. "Budget is tight." "Limited resources." "You're valued." All lies.

The company posted record profits last quarter. The CEO got a $2 million bonus. But John's "raise" is constrained by "limited resources."

"I'm now doing the work of three people with the staff cuts," John says, trying to keep his voice steady. "My workload has increased significantly."

"And I appreciate your flexibility," his boss says. "That's exactly the kind of team-player attitude we need. It's noted here." He points to the "Teamwork: Meets Expectations" line.

Noted. Not rewarded. Just noted.

John realizes this conversation is over. The number has been decided. The form has been printed. This meeting is not a negotiation. It's a notification.

"Is there anything else?" his boss asks.

John wants to scream. He wants to flip the table. He wants to tell his boss that he's a coward and a puppet and that this entire system is designed to take everything from workers and give nothing in return.

But John has a mortgage. And a car payment. And credit card debt. And kids who need shoes.

"No," John says. "Thank you."

He signs the form. His boss signs the form. They shake hands. John walks back to his cubicle.

$110 per month. After four years of sacrifice.

At his desk, he stares at his computer screen. He feels hollow. He feels used.

He feels exactly like what he is: a slave who was just told his value.

But he can't quit. He can't even consider quitting. Because the system is designed to prevent escape. The mortgage, the car payment, the debt, they're all chains that keep him locked in place.

This is Thursday.

Two more hours until he can go home. Three hundred and sixty-four more days until the next performance review.

John gets back to work.

FRIDAY: THE PAYCHECK THAT'S ALREADY SPENT

Friday morning. 5:45 AM. The alarm goes off, and John hits snooze. Just a few more minutes. He deserves just a few more minutes after yesterday's humiliation.

At 5:54 AM, the alarm goes off again. He drags himself out of bed.

It's Friday. Payday. The day everyone at the office pretends to be excited about. "Happy Friday!" people say in the hallways, as if Friday is somehow different from Monday. As if the paycheck they're about to receive isn't already spent before it hits their account.

John checks his bank account while he's drinking his coffee. His paycheck will deposit tonight at midnight. $2,305.
But it's already gone:

- Mortgage payment (auto-draft): $2,400
- Car payment (auto-draft): $389
- Student loan (auto-draft): $380
- Credit card minimum payment: $240

Total auto-withdrawals: $3,409
His paycheck: $2,305

He's $1,104 short. Again.

This is how it works every two weeks. His paycheck arrives and disappears simultaneously. The money passes through his account like water through a strainer. He never actually possesses it. He's just the middleman between his employer and his creditors.
Sarah's paycheck will cover some of the gap. Her $1,400 biweekly check will cover groceries, utilities, gas, and the kids' expenses. But there's still a shortfall. There's always a shortfall.

The credit card balance continues to grow.

John finishes his coffee and heads to work. The commute is the same. I-71 eastbound, brake lights stretching to the horizon, NPR talking about consumer confidence and job growth and economic indicators that have nothing to do with John's reality.
When he arrives at work, his coworkers are in slightly better moods. It's Friday. The weekend is coming. Two days of "freedom" before the cycle starts again.

THE TYRANT

Except the weekend isn't free. On Saturday, John has to mow the lawn, clean the gutters, fix the leaking faucet he's been putting off, take his son to soccer practice, and shop for groceries. On Sundays, there's church (where he'll sit and pretend everything is fine), meal prep for the next week, laundry, and trying to rest before Monday arrives again. The weekend is just maintenance. Maintenance of the house he's enslaved to. Maintenance of the car he's enslaved to. Maintenance of the life he's enslaved to.

At 10 AM, John has coffee with Dave, one of his coworkers. Dave is 52 years old, been with the company for 14 years. Dave looks tired. Deep lines around his eyes. Gray hair. Shoulders permanently slumped from years of sitting at a desk.

"Did you have your review yet?" John asks.

"Yesterday," Dave says. "2.2% raise."

Dave makes $92,000 per year. His 2.2% raise is $2,024 annually. $169 per month. After taxes, maybe $120.

Dave has two kids in college. His daughter is at Ohio State; his son is at Columbus State. Between the two of them, he's paying $3,200 per month in tuition, room, and board, and that's after financial aid and the kids working part-time jobs.

Dave is drowning. He works 55 hours per week. He hasn't taken a vacation in three years. He's 52 years old and he'll work until he's 67 (if he lives that long) and then maybe, maybe, he'll get to retire with a Social Security check that covers half his expenses and a 401(k) that lost 30% of its value in the last market crash.

This is what John has to look forward to. Fourteen more years of this, and he'll be Dave. Another fifteen years after that, and maybe he'll get to stop.

"You okay?" John asks.

"Yeah," Dave lies. "Just tired. Happy it's Friday."

They both know he's not okay. They both know "happy it's Friday" is something people say to avoid talking about how they really feel.

After lunch, urgent emails and last-minute requests consume John's afternoon. His boss needs a report by the end of the day. A client needs an updated proposal. Another department needs his input on a project. Everything is urgent. Everything is due immediately. Nothing can wait until Monday.

By 4 PM, John had been working for nine hours straight. He hasn't moved from his desk except to use the bathroom. His back hurts. His eyes hurt from staring at screens. His head hurts from the fluorescent lights.

He looks around the office. Everyone looks the same. Tired. Worn down. Going through the motions.

This is what the tyrant has created: an entire workforce of people too exhausted to question why they're exhausted.

At 4:30 PM, John's boss walks by his cubicle. "Have a good weekend, John. See you Monday."

"You too," John says automatically.

He packs up his laptop, grabs his jacket, and walks to the parking lot. It's raining in Columbus. He sits in his car for a moment before starting the engine, watching the rain streak down the windshield.

The paycheck will hit his account in seven hours. And it will be gone in seven seconds as the auto-payments process.

He starts the car and drives home.

Tomorrow is Saturday. The weekend. Two days before it all starts again.

THE WEEKEND: THE ILLUSION OF FREEDOM

On Saturday morning, John sleeps in until 7:30 AM. This is his "sleeping in." Eight and a half hours of sleep. The most he's gotten all week. His body is so conditioned to wake up early that even on weekends, he can't sleep past 7:30.

THE TYRANT

He lies in bed for ten minutes scrolling through his phone. Social media. Everyone posts their highlight reels. A former college friend just bought a boat. A coworker is on vacation in Hawaii. His cousin posted photos of his new house, a 4-bedroom with a pool.

John feels a familiar twist in his gut. Comparison. Envy. The quiet whisper: "Why don't I have those things? What am I doing wrong?"

He doesn't realize he's watching carefully curated lies of deceit. The friend with the boat is $85,000 in debt. The coworker in Hawaii put the entire trip on credit cards. The cousin with the new house works 70 hours a week and hasn't seen his kids awake in three months.

But John doesn't see that. He only sees what they want him to see. And it makes him feel like he's failing.

This is the tyrant's work. Keep you comparing. Encourage you to strive for things of this world. Keep you believing that if you just work a little harder, sacrifice a little more, you can have what they have. Never let you realize that "they" are just as enslaved as you are.

At 8 AM, John gets out of bed. Sarah is already up, making breakfast for the kids. Pancakes. The kids are happy. This is the closest thing to peace John will feel all day.

After breakfast, the list of tasks begins.

8:30 AM - Mow the lawn. The grass is getting long. The HOA has a policy: grass cannot exceed 4 inches. John's is at 3.5 inches. If he waits another week, he'll get a violation notice. A warning first, then a $50 fine, then a $100 fine, escalating from there.

The HOA (Homeowners Association) is another layer of rules. Another set of regulations. Another entity extracting money through fines and fees. John pays $75 per month in HOA dues. That's $900 per year for the privilege of having strangers tell him how tall his grass can be, what color he can paint his house, and whether he can park his car on the street overnight.

He mows. It takes an hour. The mower is running low on gas. He'll need to stop at the gas station later and fill up the 2-gallon can. That's another $8.

9:45 AM - Clean the gutters. It's been raining a lot, and the gutters are full of leaves and debris. If he doesn't clean them, water will overflow and eventually damage the roof. Then he'll need a new roof, which costs $15,000.

He climbs the ladder, pulls handfuls of wet, rotting leaves out of the gutters, and dumps them in a trash bag. It takes 45 minutes. His back hurts. He's not as young as he used to be. He's 38 years old, and his body already feels like it's breaking down from stress and lack of sleep.

10:45 AM - Fix the leaking faucet. He's been putting this off for three weeks. It's just a slow drip, but it's wasting water (which he pays for), and it's annoying at night when the house is quiet.

He goes to the Home Depot. The trip takes 40 minutes round-trip. The replacement parts cost $18. He could have called a plumber, but that would cost a minimum of $150. So, he does it himself. It takes him an hour to figure it out, following a YouTube video on his phone. He gets it done. The faucet stops dripping.

He just "saved" $132 by not calling a plumber. But he spent 90 minutes of his Saturday doing work he doesn't want to do. What is his time worth? If he makes $75,000 per year working 2,080 hours, his time is worth $36 per hour. He just spent $54 worth of his time to save $132. But that math doesn't work for John because John doesn't have $132. So he trades his time instead. Time he'll never get back. Time he could have spent with his kids.

12:30 PM - Lunch. Sarah makes sandwiches. The kids are arguing about something. John is too tired to care. He eats in silence.

1:00 PM - Take his son to soccer practice. His son is 8 years old and plays in the local youth soccer league. Practice is every Saturday from 1:30 to 3:00 PM.

The league costs $200 per season. The price of the uniform is $85. The cleats cost $45. Along with shin guards, a ball, and water, another $40. Total cost: $370 for a season of youth soccer.

But it's "good for him," everyone says. "Kids need activities." "It teaches teamwork and discipline."

It truly teaches that people must exploit even childhood for money. Even the tyrant has capitalized on play. Someone is making money off John's son running around a field kicking a ball.

John sits on the sidelines with the other parents. They make small talk. Someone mentions a vacation they're planning to Mexico. Someone else talks about renovating their kitchen. John nods and smiles and says nothing about the fact that he can barely afford groceries.

This is the performance everyone puts on. Everyone pretending they're fine. Everyone hides their debt, their stress, their fear.

3:15 PM - Grocery shopping. After soccer, John and Sarah take the kids to the grocery store. They need food for the next week. Sarah has a list. She's organized. Coupons and the store app help her get discounts when she shops. She's trying to keep the bill under $150.

They walk through the aisles. Everything is more expensive than it was six months ago. Milk is up 15%. Eggs are up 25%. Chicken is up 20%. Sarah adjusts her list as they go, putting things back, choosing cheaper alternatives.

The kids ask for treats: cookies, chips, soda. Sarah says yes to one thing. The kids complain it's not fair that they can't have everything they want.

John doesn't say what he's thinking: "Neither can I."

The total at checkout: $167. More than they had budgeted. It's always more.

4:30 PM - Home. Sarah starts meal prepping for the week. She cooks chicken breasts, portions them into containers, chops vegetables, and makes a big batch of rice. This is how they save money: prepare meals in advance so they're not tempted to order takeout during the week.

John helps by entertaining the kids. They play board games. They watch a movie. This is the best part of his Saturday. Two hours of just being present with his children.

But in the back of his mind, he's thinking about Sunday. About the lawn that needs edging. About the bills that need to be paid online. About the work emails he should probably check. About Monday morning coming in 36 hours.

7:00 PM - Dinner. They eat together as a family. Grilled chicken, steamed broccoli, rice. Simple. Healthy. Cheap.

8:00 PM - Kids' bedtime routine. Bath, teeth, stories, prayers. John reads to his daughter. She's reading at a seventh-grade level even though she's in 5th grade. She's smart. She's going to do great things. John believes this.

But he also knows the system will try to break her the way it's breaking him. The system will tell her to get good grades to get into a good college, which will lead to a good job, and then she will be enslaved, just like her father.

And John doesn't know how to protect her from that.

9:00 PM - John's "free time." Sarah is exhausted and goes to bed. John sits on the couch with his laptop. He should relax. He should watch something mindless on Netflix. He should just exist for an hour without being productive.

But he can't. His mind is racing. He checks his work email. Seventeen new emails since he left the office yesterday. Three of them are from his boss. None of them urgent, but all of them demanding his attention.

He responds to two of them. He shouldn't. It's Saturday night. But if he doesn't, they'll be waiting for him Monday morning, and Monday is already going to be overwhelming.

This is the trap. The work never ends. Even on your "days off," you're working. Preparing. Planning. Thinking. Stressing.

THE TYRANT

10:30 PM - Bed. John sets his alarm for 7:00 AM. He'll sleep for eight hours. Better than weeknights. But still not enough to recover from the week he just endured.

SUNDAY: THE DAY OF FALSE REST

Sunday morning. 7:00 AM.

John wakes without an alarm. His body has learned the rhythm.

Sarah is already up. She's getting the kids ready for church. They go to a mid-sized evangelical church about 15 minutes away. They've been attending for three years.

Church is supposed to be a place of rest, of worship, of community. But for John, it's become another obligation. Another place where he has to perform. Another place where he has to pretend everything is fine.

9:00 AM - Church service. They arrived ten minutes early. Sarah takes the kids to their Sunday school classes. John finds a seat in the sanctuary.

The service starts with worship music. The band plays contemporary Christian songs, loud, energetic, designed to make you feel something. John stands and sings along, but his mind is elsewhere. He's thinking about the credit card bill that's due next week. The $8,400 balance that keeps growing.

The pastor preaches a sermon about God's provision. About trusting God with your finances. About how God will supply all your needs according to His riches in glory.

John wants to believe this. He desperately wants to believe this.

But he's been trusting God with his finances for years, and he's deeper in debt every month. He's been praying for provision, and the only provision he gets is a 2.5% raise that doesn't keep up with inflation.

Someone is passing the offering plate around. John feels guilt beginning to well up deep inside. He knows that whatever he gives will have to be covered by the credit card somewhere else. "God doesn't want me to go deeper into debt to give, right?" he thinks to himself.

As the plate gets closer, his palms begin to sweat. Everyone will know he doesn't give to the church if it passes by and he does nothing. "Ah! I have a $5 bill in my pocket," he remembers. His saving grace. He palms the money so nobody can see how little he is giving and places it in the offering plate.

The sermon ends with an altar call for anyone struggling financially. "Come forward and let us pray for you," the pastor says.

John doesn't go forward. He can't. If he goes forward, everyone will know he's struggling. And John has spent years building a facade that he's fine. He can't let that crack now. He can't allow people to see the truth.

After the service, there's coffee and donuts in the fellowship hall. People mingle. They ask how you're doing. You say, "Good, how are you?" They say, "Good." Everyone is lying.

John talks to Mike, a guy from his small group. Mike works in tech, makes six figures, and drives a Tesla. Mike is talking about a mission trip he's planning to Guatemala. $2,500 per person for a week.

John will never go on a mission trip. He can't afford it.

"You should come," Mike says. "It's life-changing."

"Maybe," John says. "We'll see."

Mike doesn't know that "we'll see" means "no."

11:30 AM - Home. The kids are hungry. Sarah makes lunch: sandwiches again. John is tiring of sandwiches.

12:30 PM - Laundry. Six loads. Wash, dry, fold, put away. This takes three hours. Sarah and John work together, assembly-line style. It's tedious. It's mindless. It's necessary.

While the laundry runs, John pays bills online. He logs into his bank account and starts clicking through payments:
· Electric: $128 (up from $115 last month)
· Water: $65
· Internet: $80
· Cell phones (family plan): $180

28

· Netflix: $15
· Hulu: $13
· Disney+: $8 (for the kids)

The subscriptions alone are $36 per month. That's $432 per year for streaming services. John doesn't even watch most of it. But the kids do. And canceling would mean dealing with their complaints.

He moves money around. Transfers $200 from savings to checking to cover the shortfall from this week's bills. His savings account now has $197. His "emergency fund" couldn't cover a single emergency.

3:30 PM - Meal prep continues. Sarah is making a big pot of chili for the week. John chops onions. They work in silence. They're both too tired to talk.

5:00 PM - Dinner. The chili is ready. They eat early. The kids don't like chili. They complain. They eat it anyway because there's no alternative.

6:00 PM - Family time. They watch a movie together. Something animated that the kids picked. John falls asleep halfway through. Sarah wakes him up when it's over.

8:00 PM - Kids' bedtime. The routine repeats. Bath, teeth, stories, prayers.

SUNDAY NIGHT: THE DREAD RETURNS

9:00 PM - The Sunday Night Dread. John is lying in bed, wide awake, staring at the ceiling. He has 47 unread emails. His four projects are behind schedule. He has a boss who expects him to do the work of three people. In two weeks, he has a mortgage payment. He has a credit card balance that's growing, and he has a car that's going to need new tires soon.

And he has no escape. No exit. No way out.

This is Sunday night. The worst night of the week. The night when the illusion of the weekend dissolves and reality crashes back in.

Sarah is already asleep. John lies there for an hour before his mind finally lets him rest.

Tomorrow is Monday.

The cycle begins again.

And again. And again. And again.

Every week, the same pattern. Work, bills, survival. John believes this is normal. He believes everyone lives this way. He believes he's doing well because he owns a house, two cars, and provides for his family.
But does he own them? Or do they own him?
I will show you something John cannot see. Let me pull back the curtain on every single transaction, every payment, every "purchase" he makes. Let me show you all the hands reaching into John's pocket.

Because John doesn't own anything. John is owned.

PART TWO: THE WEB OF GREED

If you're feeling overwhelmed, angry, or hopeless right now: good. That means you're seeing clearly. John's story isn't just numbers on a page. It's your story. And the weight of that truth should feel heavy.

Now you need to see who profits from it. Before I show you the way out, you need to understand the web.

Every Hand in Your Pocket

You think you own things. You don't. Things own you. And between you and the thing you think you own stands an entire army of greed and selfishness, each taking their cut, each living off your labor.

Let me show you exactly how deep the greed goes. Let's start with something you use every single day, something you believe gives you freedom: your car.

THE CAR: A Case Study in Systematic Greed

John drives a 2019 Honda Accord with 35,000 miles that he bought used for $24,000. Sarah drives a 2017 Toyota Camry with 48,000 miles that they bought for $18,000. He thinks he's being "financially responsible" buying used Japanese cars. Between the two cars, this family is deeply enslaved.

Let's trace John's Honda to show how deep the greed goes. Sarah's car follows the same pattern.

Let's trace every single hand that reached into John's pocket to extract wealth from this "responsible" purchase.

Layer 1: The Original Manufacturing
Honda Motor Company (Japan)
· Manufacturing cost per Accord: approximately $18,000
· Sells to distributor for: $28,500
· Honda's gross profit: $10,500 per vehicle.

Before the car ever touches American soil, Honda has extracted $10,500 in profit. But Honda is just the beginning.

Parts Suppliers Honda doesn't make every part. They assemble parts made by hundreds of suppliers: Denso, Aisin, Takata, Bridgestone and NGK. Each extracting a 15-30% markup on components sold to Honda. Supplier markups already inflated the "manufacturing cost" of $18,000.

Raw Materials
They extract steel, aluminum, rubber, petroleum, and rare earth minerals from the earth (resources that were a free gift from God), sell them to refiners who mark them up, who sell to parts suppliers who mark them up again, who sell to manufacturers who mark them up once more.

Labor Exploitation
Assembly workers earn $28/hour building a $28,500 car. They receive a tiny fraction; executives and shareholders take the rest.

Layer 2: Import and Distribution
Shipping Companies
They must transport the car from Japan to the United States.
· Ocean freight: $800 per vehicle
· Port fees: $250
· Customs processing: $150
· Inland transport to dealership: $400
Total transportation cost: $1,600

But the shipping company didn't pay $1,600 to move the car. Their actual cost (fuel, labor, ship maintenance) is approximately $600. They're extracting $850 in profit per vehicle.

Import Duties and Taxes

The U.S. government charges a 2.5% tariff on imported passenger vehicles:

· 2.5% of $28,500 = $712.50

The government extracted $712.50 for the privilege of allowing a car to enter the country. They did no work. No value was created by them. They just collected a fee because they control the border.

Regional Distributor

Honda doesn't sell directly to dealerships. They sell to regional distributors, who then sell to dealerships:

· Distributor buys from Honda: $28,500
· Distributor sells to dealership: $31,000
· Distributor's markup: $2,500

The distributor adds no value to the car. They're a middleman taking a piece of the pie.

Layer 3: The Dealership (First Sale)

The dealership bought the car from the distributor for $31,500. They sold it new in 2019 for $38,500.

Dealer Markup: $7,000

But wait, there's more:

Dealer Preparation Fee:

- $895 This covers washing the car and removing the plastic from the seats.

Cost to dealer: $75.
Profit: $820.
Documentation Fee:

- $599 This covers the paperwork.

Cost to dealer: $40 in actual paper and ink.
Profit: $559.
Extended Warranty (sold to original buyer):

- $2,400 Actual cost of warranty to dealer: $900.

Profit: $1,500.
Paint Protection/Fabric Protection:

- $1,200

Actual cost: $150 in chemicals and labor.
Profit: $1,050.
Total dealer profit on first sale: $11,929
The dealership extracted $11,929 for being a second middleman between Honda and the customer. They added no value to the car. They just controlled access to a new vehicle.
Dealership Salesperson Commission:

- $900 (approximately 7–8% of gross profit)

The salesperson who spent 2 hours with the customer gets $900. The dealership owners get the rest.
Finance Manager Profit:
The original buyer financed through the dealership at 4.9% APR. The bank was willing to approve at 3.9%, but the dealership marked it up and kept the difference.
Markup profit over the life of the loan: $1,000
First Owner's Sales Tax and Government Fees:
But the government gets its cut of the $38,500 sales price.
Ohio charges a 5.75% sales tax on new vehicle purchases:

- Sales tax on $38,500: $2,213.75

Plus government fees:

- Title fee: $93
- Registration (first year): $225
- Plate fee: $21.50

Total government taking on first sale: $2,553.25

The first owner paid $41,053.25 out the door for a car the dealership acquired for $31,500.
$9,553.25 was taken at the point of sale: $7,000 in immediate dealer markup and $2,553.25 in government taxes and fees.

But that was only the beginning. Through add-ons, warranties, and finance rate markups rolled into the loan, the dealership locked in an additional $4,929 in gross profit, bringing **total dealer profit on this single transaction to $11,929.**

Layer 4: The First Owner (2019–2022)
The original owner drove the car for three years and 35,000 miles. Then they sold it.
In those three years, the original owner paid:

- Purchase price (including fees and tax): $41,053.25
- Interest paid during first 36 months: ~$3,400
- Insurance: $4,950
- Gas: $6,600
- Maintenance (oil, tires, rotations): $1,310
- Registration (years 2–3): $450

Total out-of-pocket cost (before trade-in): ~$57,763
The original owner drove 35,000 miles.

That's $1.65 per mile. More expensive than Uber. And they still didn't own the car.

Layer 5: The Used Car Auction
The original owner traded the car in to a dealership when buying their next vehicle. The dealership gave them $18,000 trade-in value (the car was worth $22,000 retail, but trade-in values are always lower).
But the dealership doesn't sell it on its lot. They send it to auction.
Manheim Auto Auction: Charges a $300 seller fee and a $400 buyer fee, extracting $700 for facilitating the transaction.
The car sold at auction for $19,500. After Manheim's seller fee, the first dealership nets $19,200. Since they paid the original owner $18,000, the dealership pockets a $1,200 profit.
The second dealership pays $19,900 to acquire the car.

Layer 6: The Second Dealership
This is where John enters the picture.
The dealership bought the car at auction for $19,900 and added their minimal reconditioning costs:

- Detailing: $125
- 120-point inspection: $75
- Minor scratch repair: $150

Total actual investment: $20,250

They listed the car for **$26,500**, but John negotiated them down to $24,000. He felt like he won. He got them to come down $2,500.
Then the dealership added the junk fees:

- Documentation fee: $599
- Dealer prep fee: $395

John's actual price before taxes: $24,994
$24,994 − $20,250 = $4,744 profit for the dealership

Layer 7: Sales Tax and Government Fees
Ohio charges a 5.75% sales tax on used vehicles:

- Sales tax on $24,000: $1,380

Plus additional fees:

- Title fee: $93
- Registration: $122
- Plate fee: $21.50

Total government take: $1,616.50
(The government has now taken $4,169.75 out of the same vehicle.)
Total out the door: $26,610.50
At signing, John put $4,000 down and paid the $994 in dealer fees plus $1,616.50 in taxes and government charges out of pocket, financing only the remaining $20,000.

Layer 8: The Ongoing Greed
Now the real bleeding begins. John doesn't pay just once for the car. He pays every single month, every single year, for the privilege of driving it.
Financing: John financed $20,000 at 6.5% APR for 60 months.

- Monthly payment: $391.32
- Total payments over 5 years: $23,479.20
- Interest paid to the bank: $3,479.20

The bank created money out of nothing (fractional reserve banking), loaned it to John, and will collect $3,479.20 in pure profit. But it gets better. The bank didn't actually loan its own money. They borrowed it from the Federal Reserve at 2% and loaned it to John at 6.5%. They're making a 4.5% profit on money that isn't even theirs.

Insurance: John pays $180/month for car insurance. That's $2,160 per year. Over the 5 years he'll own the car, that's $10,800.

John's insurance company has collected from him for 2 years so far: $4,320. They've paid out: $0. John hasn't had any accidents.

The insurance company's actual cost for covering John is approximately $35/month. They're taking $145/month in profit. Over 5 years: $8,700 in profit from John alone.

State Farm's CEO earned $19.2 million in 2023. That money came from John and millions like him.

Gas: John drives approximately 12,000 miles per year. His Accord gets 30 MPG. That's 400 gallons per year at $3.89 per gallon. Total: $1,556 per year, or $7,780 over 5 years.

Of that $3.89/gallon: crude oil $1.85, refining $0.65, distribution $0.45, station markup $0.25, taxes $0.69.

The government takes $276/year from John's gas purchases alone.

Maintenance: Oil changes, tires, brakes, filters total $2,320 over 5 years.

Actual cost to shops: $948.

Profit taken: $1,372.

Registration: John pays $122 per year to renew his registration. That's $610 over 5 years. The actual cost to the state for processing his paperwork: approximately $8.

Government taking: $570 over 5 years.

Depreciation: When John bought the car in 2022, it was worth $24,000. When he sells it in 2027, it will be worth approximately $12,000. Loss in value: $12,000. This isn't money John paid to anyone directly, but it's value that evaporated. The car lost half its value just by existing and aging.

THE TOTAL GREED FROM JOHN'S CAR

Let's add it all up. How much will John's "responsible" used car purchase actually cost him over 5 years of ownership?
Initial purchase:

- Down payment: $4,000
- Loan payments: $23,479.20
- Fees and taxes: $1,616.50

Ongoing costs:

- Insurance: $10,800
- Gas: $7,780
- Maintenance: $2,320
- Registration: $610
- Total cash outflow: $50,605.70
- Plus depreciation: $12,000

Total cost of ownership: **$62,605.70**

John will spend $50,605.70 in cash and lose an additional $12,000 in value, for a total cost of $62,605.70 over five years.

Now let's trace the greed:
Who profited from John's car?

- Honda (original manufacturing): $10,500
- Parts suppliers: $3,200
- Shipping companies: $850

- U.S. Government (import tariff): $713
- Regional distributor: $2,500
- First dealership (new sale): $11,929
- Ohio Government (first owner's sales tax & fees): $2,553
- Original owner's insurance: $3,690
- Original owner's maintenance shops: $850
- Original owner's interest: $3,400
- First dealership (trade-in): $1,200
- Manheim Auction: $700
- Second dealership (John's purchase): $4,744
- Ohio Government (John's sales tax & fees): $1,617
- John's bank (interest): $3,479
- John's insurance company (profit): $8,700
- John's maintenance shops: $1,372
- Ohio DMV (registration profit): $570

Total PROFIT taken from one car and two owners: $62,567

From a car that cost $18,000 to manufacture.

This is a 348% markup from manufacturing cost to total profit extracted from the original owner through John's five years of ownership (2019-2027). And this is just one car for two families.
Multiply this by millions of families, across cars, houses, food, healthcare, education. The tyrant doesn't take from John alone. The tyrant takes from everyone systematically, relentlessly, enslaving lives for the sake of greed.
John drives to work believing his car gives him freedom. Believing he had made a smart choice in buying used. He doesn't see the 50+ entities that took wealth from this purchase. He doesn't see that his car, the symbol of American freedom, is actually a chain binding him to debt, payments, insurance, maintenance.

THE TYRANT

John doesn't work to support his car. The car is a tool to take from his life. And the tyrant always places a heavy burden on God's people.

THE PHONE

Now let's look at something smaller. Something you probably have in your pocket right now. Something you check 100+ times per day. Something you believe you can't live without.

Your phone.

John has an iPhone 13. He bought it two years ago when his iPhone 10 stopped receiving security updates and his apps stopped working. He didn't want to upgrade. He was forced to upgrade.
This shows planned failure in action.

The Purchase
Apple Store Price: $799 (128GB model)
But John didn't pay $799 upfront. He financed it through his carrier, Verizon, at $33.29/month for 24 months.
Total paid: $798.96 (essentially the same as paying cash, no interest because Verizon uses the financing to lock you into their service)

Manufacturing Cost
Apple doesn't publish its actual costs, but analysis by teardown experts estimates:

- Components: $425
- Assembly: $30
- Packaging: $5
- Shipping: $10

Total cost to manufacture: $470
Apple's profit per device: $329

But that $329 is just the beginning of Apple taking from John.

Layer 1: The Components
Apple buys components from suppliers: Samsung (display), TSMC (processor), Sony (camera), Texas Instruments, Broadcom and Qualcomm. Each extracting 50-100% profit margins before Apple even assembles the phone.

Layer 2: Rare Earth Minerals
Those chips and components require rare earth minerals mined from the earth:

Congo cobalt mining: Children as young as 7 work for $1-2/day. Cobalt sold to refiners at $15/kg, resold to manufacturers at $35/kg.

China rare earths: Controls 80% of global supply. Workers exposed to toxic chemicals for poverty wages.

Those doing the dangerous work make almost nothing. Corporations controlling the supply chain extract massive profits.

Layer 3: The Carrier (Verizon)
John's monthly phone bill: $180 (family plan for 4 lines)
Breakdown:

- Base service (4 lines): $120
- Data (30GB shared): $50
- Taxes and fees: $10
- Verizon's actual cost to provide this service to John is approximately $35/month.
- Network maintenance: $15
- Customer service overhead: $8
- Billing systems: $5
- Actual data/voice costs: $7

Verizon's monthly profit from John: $145
Annual profit: $1,740
Over 10 years of service: $17,400

Layer 4: Apple's Ongoing Greed
John didn't just buy a phone. He entered Apple's ecosystem, a system designed to collect money from him every month, indefinitely.
iCloud Storage
John pays $2.99/month for 200GB of iCloud storage.
Large-scale cloud storage costs companies **pennies per user per month** due to massive economies of scale. Independent infrastructure analyses estimate Apple's per-user storage cost at **well under $0.50/month.**
Apple charges John $35.88 per year for a service that costs them only a fraction of that to provide.
Apple Music
John pays $16.99/month for a family plan: $203.88 per year.
Artists are typically paid **fractions of a cent per stream**, and after record-label splits, only a small portion of John's subscription reaches the musicians he listens to. Most of the subscription revenue stays inside Apple's services division.
App Store Tax
Apple takes 30% of every paid app and in-app purchase. Not because they earned it through competition, but because they own the platform. You want an iPhone app? You pay Apple's tax. No alternatives. No negotiation.
AppleCare+
John paid $199 for two years of AppleCare+.
Extended warranties are among the highest-margin products in consumer electronics. Industry estimates consistently show that **only a small percentage of customers ever use AppleCare**, allowing Apple to price it far above expected repair costs.

Layer 5: Data Mining

But here's the greed you can't see, the greed that happens without you paying a single dollar directly.

Every time John uses his iPhone, his location is tracked, his searches recorded, his app usage monitored, his contacts scanned, his photos analyzed, his voice processed. This data is worth money. Lots of money. Apple's services revenue in 2023: $85.2 billion. Google pays Apple $18 billion/year to be the default search engine. Advertisers pay for targeted ads based on your data.

John's data is worth approximately $150-200 per year to various companies. Over 10 years: $1,500-2,000 of value extracted from John without him receiving a penny.

Layer 6: App Ecosystem Greed

Each "free" app is extracting value from John:

- Google Maps: Tracks every location, sells data to advertisers (~$25/year)
- Facebook/Instagram: Sells his attention to advertisers (~$60/year)
- Amazon: Dynamic pricing based on behavior (~$150/year overpayment)

Total app ecosystem greed: $235/year = $2,350 over 10 years

THE TOTAL GREED FROM JOHN'S PHONE

Over 10 years, John will pay:

- iPhone hardware (4 devices): $3,196
- Verizon service: $21,600
- Apple services (iCloud, music, warranties): $2,222
- Total cash out: $27,018

But the greed goes deeper than what John pays directly:

- His data sold to advertisers: $1,750
- App ecosystem extracting from his behavior: $2,350
- Total extracted: $31,118

Who profits:

- Apple: $1,300 per device + most of that $2,222 in services
- Verizon: $17,400 in pure profit over 10 years
- Component suppliers: $3,000 embedded in manufacturing
- Data brokers: $1,750 from selling John's information
- App platforms: $2,350 in rents and manipulation

John pays $31,118 over 10 years for devices that cost $470 to manufacture.

But here's the real horror: John believes his phone is a tool he controls. He doesn't realize:

- He's the product being sold
- Every interaction is monetized
- His attention is the commodity
- His data is more valuable than the phone itself
- The phone doesn't work for him; he works for the phone
- The phone is not a tool. The phone is a chain.

It tracks your location. It demands your attention. It requires constant payment. It collects your data. It feeds you advertisements. It creates artificial needs.

And you carry it willingly. You check it 100+ times per day. You feel anxiety when it's not near you. You have become dependent on your own anchor that drags you down.

This is the tyrant's masterpiece: a chain you pay for, a cage you carry, a system of control you defend. And we haven't even touched on the content the phone transmits into your mind and spirit.

THE MATHMATICS OF SLAVERY

Here's exactly how John's life is divided.
John makes $75,000 per year. That's $6,250 per month gross. But John never sees that number. Let's watch what happens to it:

FEDERAL GOVERNMENT TAKES FIRST:

- Federal Income Tax: ~$850/month
- Social Security: $388/month
- Medicare: $91/month

Total to Federal Government: $1,329/month (21% of his gross income)
That's approximately 4.5 days of work every month. And they take it from John before he even sees a dollar of it. Tyrant gets paid first. At all times.

STATE OF OHIO TAKES NEXT:

- State Income Tax: ~$450/month

Total to State Government: $450/month (7.2% of gross)
Add another 1.5 days of work per month for the state.
Now, John's take-home is $4,610/month. But the taking has only begun.

THE MORTGAGE ENSLAVES HIM:

- Mortgage payment (modest 3-bedroom in Columbus): $2,400/month

Of that $2,400, approximately $1,800 is interest to the bank

- Property taxes (included in mortgage): $450/month
- Homeowner's insurance: $150/month

The house alone costs John $2,400/month, which is 8.1 days of work.

Now break down that interest: $1,800/month is pure profit for the bank. That's 6.0 days per month John works just to make bankers rich. By year 12.5, John will have paid the bank $360,000, the full purchase price of the house. Yet he'll still owe them over $260,000 and won't own it free and clear for another 17.5 years.

He's not building equity; he's paying for the privilege of owing them money. By the time the mortgage ends, the bank will have collected more than **two times the value of the home**.

THE CARS ENSLAVE HIM:

- Car payments (John's Honda + Sarah's Toyota): $674/month
- Car insurance (both cars): $285/month

Total: $959/month = 3.2 days of work

GASOLINE:

- Both cars: $320/month

= 1.1 days of work

DAYCARE:

- When neither parent is available: $1,200/month

= 4.0 days of work

UTILITIES & CONNECTIVITY (required to function in society):

- Electricity: $120/month
- Natural gas (Columbus winters): $80/month
- Internet: $80/month (required for his job, mandatory)
- Cell phone (family plan): $180/month

Total: $460/month = 1.5 days of work
FOOD:

- Groceries: $500/month (he eats cheaply)

= 1.7 days of work
STUDENT LOANS (because he needed that degree to get this job):

- $380/month

= 1.3 days of work
CREDIT CARD MINIMUM PAYMENTS (the debt that keeps growing):

- $240/month

= 0.8 days of work

John's Monthly Slavery Calculation
Let's add it up. Out of approximately 21 working days per month (assuming 5-day work weeks):

- 4.5 days → Federal government
- 1.5 days → State government
- 1.5 days → Property taxes (local government)
- 6.0 days → Bank interest (the slavery of debt)
- 3.2 days → Car payments and insurance
- 1.1 days → Gasoline

- 4.0 days → Daycare
- 1.5 days → Utilities and connectivity
- 1.7 days → Food
- 1.3 days → Student loans
- 0.8 days → Credit card minimums

Total: 27.1 days of work to cover 21 working days per month.

Wait. That's more than the working days you have.

John needs to work 27.1 days. He has only 21 working days. He's 6.1 days short.

Sarah helps. She works part time and nets $1,000/month after all her costs (her car payment, insurance, gas, work expenses). That covers approximately 3.4 days of their shortfall.

Combined: 21 + 3.4 = 24.4 days of work.

But they need 27.1 days.

The gap: 2.7 days = $674 per month.

That's where the credit card comes in. And John's already paying $240/month in credit card minimums. That debt is from LAST month's shortfall. And the month before. And the month before that.

Every month, John goes $674 deeper into debt. The credit card minimum he's paying today is just servicing the debt he couldn't afford to pay in previous months. And this month's $674 shortfall? That becomes next month's growing balance, with interest compounding on top.

The hole keeps getting deeper.

John has NEGATIVE freedom. He's not just enslaved; he's drowning. And Sarah's working herself to exhaustion just to slow the drowning, not stop it.

THE LIFETIME CALCULATION

Let's zoom out. Let's look at John's entire working life.

John is 38 years old. He'll work until he's 67 (if Social Security still exists by then). That's 29 more years of this.

29 years × 12 months = 348 months remaining

Here's what John will pay over the rest of his working life:

To the Federal Government:

- $1,329/month × 348 months = $462,492

To the State Government:

- $450/month × 348 months = $156,600

To Banks (interest only):

- Mortgage interest: $1,800/month × 324 months (27 years remaining) = $583,200
- Car loan interest: $200/month average × 348 months = $69,600
- Student loan interest: $180/month × 144 months (12 years remaining) = $25,920
- Credit card interest: $120/month average × 348 months = $41,760

Total bank interest: $720,480

Let's add it up:

Over his remaining working life, John will pay:

- Federal government: $462,492
- State government: $156,600
- Banks (interest only): $720,480

Total taken from John: $1,339,572
(Note: We include property taxes in the mortgage payment rather than counting them separately.)
John's total gross earnings over 29 years:
$75,000/year × 29 years = $2,175,000
Yes, John will get small raises over those 29 years. But inflation will eat them. His purchasing power will stay roughly flat, maybe decline. So this math holds.
$1,339,572 taken from $2,175,000 earned = 62% of his gross income
62% of everything John earns goes to the government and bank interest. And that's BEFORE we count:

- The principal on his mortgage (the actual house cost)
- The principal of his cars
- Insurance companies
- Utility companies
- Gas companies
- Food markups
- Every other hand in his pocket

Nearly two-thirds of John's entire working life, taken before he can even think about survival. Gone. Not building anything. Not creating anything. Just transferred to others who offered him the privilege of living "free".

THE COST OF BORROWED MONEY
Let's look closer at the $720,480 in interest John will pay to banks over his lifetime.

Interest is money paid for money that didn't exist until the bank created it on a computer. The bank didn't earn this money. The bank didn't work for this money. The bank typed numbers into a system and now owns 9.6 years of John's entire working life.

$720,480 in interest payments = 9.6 years of John's gross income

Think about that. 9.6 years of waking up, driving to work, sitting in meetings, responding to emails, dealing with his boss, sacrificing time with his family. All of that labor, all of that life, converted into interest payments to banks.

John won't build meaningful equity with this money. He won't feed his family with it. He won't enjoy it. It's pure greed. Pure enslavement.

The bank sucks its wealth from John's life, one payment at a time.

THE PRICE OF EXISTENCE

Here's the question that reveals everything: After all the mandatory payments, how much of John's life is actually his?

Working days remaining in John's life: 260 days/year × 29 years = 7,540 working days

Let's calculate what gets claimed:

Government takes (federal + state):

$619,092 ÷ $2,175,000 = 28.5% of his working life

28.5% × 7,540 days = 2,149 working days

2,149 working days = 8.3 working years

Banks take (interest only):

$720,480 ÷ $2,175,000 = 33.1% of his working life

33.1% × 7,540 days = 2,496 working days

2,496 working days = 9.6 working years

Mandatory survival (principal payments on house, cars, food, utilities):

- Mortgage principal: ~$600/month × 324 months = $194,400
- Car principal: ~$474/month × 348 months = $164,952
- Food: $500/month × 348 months = $174,000
- Utilities: $460/month × 348 months = $160,080

Total mandatory survival: $693,432
$693,432 ÷ $2,175,000 = 31.9% of his working life
31.9% × 7,540 days = 2,405 working days
2,405 working days = 9.3 working years
Total days claimed: 2,149 + 2,496 + 2,405 = 7,050 working days (27.1 years)

Days John works for himself: 7,540 - 7,050 = 490 working days (1.9 years)

Out of 29 years of work, John gets to keep the fruit of his labor for 1.9 years. Everything else goes to the government, banks, and basic survival.

That's 6.5% of his working life that actually belongs to him. 93.5% of John's working life is already claimed by the tryant.

And that 6.5% "freedom"? That still has to cover:

- Student loan principal (not interest - we already counted that)
- Credit card principal
- Gas for both cars
- Car maintenance and repairs
- House maintenance and repairs
- Clothing

- Medical expenses not covered by insurance
- Insurance premiums (home, auto, health)
- Everything else

Once you factor those in, John has nothing. Zero. His entire life is spoken for before he earns a single dollar.

This is not freedom. This is not even slavery with occasional rest. This is total bondage with the illusion of choice.

And John believes he's free because he gets to choose which car to buy, which house to rent from the bank, which job to show up to.

The tyrant has perfected enslavement: Make the slave think he's free while taking everything from his life.

This is John's life. This is your life. This is everyone's life.

But John doesn't see it. Neither do you. You are blind to the truth, and this is not by accident.

How could so many factors align to enslave one person? Random chance, you believe? Thousands have coordinated to take from John's life. Thousands! This could not be coordinated by any man. This is an absolute coordinated effort by darkness.

You've seen how greed extracts wealth from John at every transaction. But greed alone cannot sustain this system. Greed needs enforcement. Greed needs control. Greed needs laws to make compliance inevitable.

Laws are what keep John compliant. Laws are another cage he cannot see.

PART THREE: THE INVISIBLE PRISON

A DAY OF LAWS

I'm going to show you something you've probably never noticed. I'm going to count every single law, regulation, and rule that governs John's life in a single day. From the moment he wakes until the moment he sleeps, thousands of rules surround him he must obey, or face punishment.

This is not freedom. This is enslavement so ingrained that you don't even see the bars.

6:00 AM - WAKING UP

John's alarm goes off. The alarm clock itself is governed by:

- Federal Communications Commission (FCC) regulations on electromagnetic interference
- Consumer Product Safety Commission (CPSC) standards for electrical devices
- Underwriters Laboratories (UL) certification requirements
- Department of Energy efficiency standards

Four regulatory bodies govern the device that wakes him up.

John checks his phone. This device is subject to:

- FCC licensing and spectrum regulations
- Federal Trade Commission (FTC) consumer protection rules
- Communications Decency Act provisions

- Digital Millennium Copyright Act restrictions
- Children's Online Privacy Protection Act (if applicable)
- State consumer protection laws
- Local 911 service requirements
- International import regulations
- Patent law protections (thousands of patents in one device)
- Intellectual property licensing agreements

Ten major regulatory frameworks govern the phone in his hand. And he hasn't gotten out of bed yet.

6:10 AM - GETTING READY

John's alarm went off at 6:00 AM. He's been awake for 10 minutes, and already he's moved through a minefield of regulations governing the simplest acts of being human.

The Bathroom

John uses the toilet. This porcelain fixture must comply with:

- Federal Energy Policy Act of 1992 (maximum 1.6 gallons per flush)
- Americans with Disabilities Act (ADA) height and clearance requirements
- Uniform Plumbing Code (UPC) installation standards
- International Residential Code (IRC) ventilation requirements
- Local plumbing codes
- Water conservation mandates

He turns on the faucet. The following regulates the water flowing through it:

- Safe Drinking Water Act (EPA standards for 90+ contaminants)
- Lead and Copper Rule (maximum allowable levels)

- Water fluoridation requirements (state-mandated in Ohio)
- Backflow prevention regulations
- Cross-connection control standards
- Maximum flow rate requirements (2.2 gallons per minute federal standard)

He brushes his teeth with toothpaste regulated by the FDA as a drug. The toothbrush is a consumer product subject to CPSC safety standards. His towel needs to meet flammability standards. The light above the mirror must meet electrical codes. The mirror itself must meet safety glazing standards to prevent shattering.

In five minutes in the bathroom, John has interacted with approximately 40 regulations. He hasn't even gotten dressed yet.

Getting Dressed

The clothes John puts on are subject to:

- Flammable Fabrics Act (pajamas, children's sleepwear must meet strict standards)
- Textile Fiber Products Identification Act (labels must disclose fiber content)
- Care Labeling Rule (washing instructions required)
- Country of Origin labeling requirements
- Formaldehyde limits in fabrics
- Lead content restrictions
- Azo dye restrictions

His shirt was manufactured overseas under trade agreements that dictate tariffs, quotas, and labor standards. The cotton was grown under agricultural regulations. Manufacturers produced the synthetic fibers under chemical manufacturing standards. Environmental agencies approved the dyes used.

Every thread on John's body has passed through a regulatory gauntlet before reaching his closet.

Breakfast

John goes downstairs and makes coffee. The coffee maker is subject to:

- UL (Underwriters Laboratories) electrical safety certification
- Energy Star efficiency requirements
- Consumer Product Safety Commission standards
- Electromagnetic interference regulations
- Fire safety standards
- Automatic shut-off requirements

Regulations govern the coffee itself:

- FDA food safety standards
- Fair Trade certification requirements (if applicable)
- Organic certification standards (if applicable)
- Pesticide residue limits
- Import regulations and tariffs
- Labeling requirements (country of origin, roast date, allergen warnings)

He pours milk into his coffee. That milk is one of the most heavily regulated foods in America.

- Pasteurization required by FDA
- Grade A standards (bacteria count, temperature, somatic cell count)
- Vitamin D fortification mandated
- Hormone labeling (rBST-free claims regulated)
- Expiration date requirements
- Storage temperature requirements
- Dairy farm inspections (monthly in most states)

The cereal box sitting on John's counter has been approved by:

- FDA nutrition labeling requirements (Nutrition Facts panel format)
- Ingredient disclosure requirements
- Allergen labeling requirements (contains wheat, manufactured in a facility with nuts)
- Health claims regulations (what can and cannot be stated)
- Serving size standardization
- Fortification requirements (vitamins and minerals added)

The bowl, the spoon, the table, the chair; every item in John's kitchen has been manufactured under safety standards, imported under trade regulations, and sold under consumer protection laws.

By 6:30 AM, John has encountered approximately 85 regulatory touchpoints while simply waking up, using the bathroom, getting dressed, and eating breakfast.

He hasn't left his house yet. He hasn't gone to work. He hasn't driven a car, or bought anything, or interacted with another human being.

He's just existed. And existence itself is regulated.

The water he drinks. The clothes he wears. The food he eats. The air he breathes (ventilation standards). The light he sees by (electrical codes). The temperature he's comfortable at (HVAC regulations). The products he touches (consumer safety).

Nothing is exempt. Nothing is free. Nothing is his choice alone.

This is what it means to wake up in the tyrant's world.

6:30 AM - LEAVING THE HOUSE

John walks out his front door. His house itself is subject to **tens of thousands of regulations**:

- Building Code (500+ pages)
- Residential Code (700+ pages)
- National Electrical Code (900+ pages)
- Plumbing Code (400+ pages)
- Mechanical Code (300+ pages)
- Energy Conservation Code
- State building codes
- Local zoning ordinances
- Homeowners Association rules (75 pages in John's case)
- Fire safety codes
- ADA accessibility requirements

John's house is subject to **at least 15,000 distinct code requirements** before he even walks out the door.

6:35 AM - THE DRIVEWAY

John walks to his car parked in his driveway. Even this is regulated:

- Parking on the driveway (not the street overnight, city ordinance)
- Driveway width requirements
- Driveway slope requirements
- Impervious surface limitations
- Stormwater management regulations

6:40 AM - DRIVING TO WORK

John backs out of his driveway and begins his commute. For the next 20 minutes, he will be subject to more regulations per minute than any other part of his day.

The Vehicle Itself

John's 2019 Honda Accord must comply with approximately 75 Federal Motor Vehicle Safety Standards (FMVSS). These aren't suggestions. These are mandatory requirements, each carrying penalties for non-compliance:

- Seat belts (FMVSS 209, 210)
- Airbags (FMVSS 208)
- Braking systems (FMVSS 105, 135)
- Lighting and reflectors (FMVSS 108)
- Fuel system integrity (FMVSS 301)
- Roof crush resistance (FMVSS 216)
- Electronic stability control (FMVSS 126)

Federal mandate regulates every component, from the rearview mirror to the exhaust system. The car cannot be manufactured, sold, or legally operated without compliance.

But the vehicle regulations are just the beginning.

The Road

John drives on roads governed by:

- Federal Highway Administration (FHWA) design standards
- Ohio Department of Transportation (ODOT) specifications
- Franklin County road maintenance codes
- Columbus Municipal Code traffic regulations
- Manual on Uniform Traffic Control Devices (MUTCD) - the federal standard for all traffic signs, signals, and markings

Every line painted on the road, every sign posted, every signal installed must comply with MUTCD specifications. The width of the lane, the curve of the road, the angle of the intersection, all are regulated.

The Driver

John himself is regulated:

- Must possess valid driver's license (Ohio Revised Code 4507)
- Must maintain minimum insurance coverage ($25,000/$50,000/$25,000)
- Must obey all traffic laws (Ohio Revised Code Chapter 4511)

- Subject to blood alcohol limit (0.08% BAC)
- Subject to traffic camera enforcement
- Subject to police observation and enforcement

Every Movement Controlled

At 6:46 AM, John encounters a stop sign. This single octagonal piece of metal represents:

- Federal MUTCD requirements (size, color, reflectivity, placement height)
- State statute requiring full stop (ORC 4511.43)
- Municipal enforcement authority
- $150 fine for rolling through
- Points on driving record
- Potential insurance rate increase
- Traffic cameras that may be recording

John stops completely. Not because he wants to. Not because there's oncoming traffic. Because the law requires it, and disobedience carries punishment.

At 6:49 AM, he drives through a school zone. The speed limit drops from 35 mph to 20 mph. This zone is governed by:

- Federal school zone designation requirements
- State school zone speed laws (ORC 4511.21)
- Enhanced penalties for violations in school zones (double fines)
- Flashing lights controlled by timer or manual operation
- School zone signage requirements
- Crossing guard regulations
- Pedestrian right-of-way laws

John slows to 20 mph. There are no children present. School doesn't start for another hour. But the flashing lights are on, so the law applies. He drives 20 mph in an empty zone because the regulation demands it. **6:51 AM**, John merges onto I-71. Now he's subject to:

- Federal Interstate Highway System regulations
- FHWA design and safety standards
- State highway patrol jurisdiction
- Posted speed limits (ORC 4511.21)
- Lane usage laws (ORC 4511.25)
- Following distance requirements (ORC 4511.34)
- Work zone regulations (when applicable)
- HOV lane restrictions (in some states)
- Truck lane restrictions (when applicable)
- Minimum speed requirements

He cannot drive too fast. He cannot drive too slow. He cannot follow too closely. He cannot change lanes improperly. He cannot use his phone. He cannot be distracted. Every action is prescribed; every violation is punishable.

The Count During This Commute

In 20 minutes of driving, John is subject to approximately:

- 75 Federal Motor Vehicle Safety Standards (vehicle)
- 40+ Federal Highway Administration regulations (roads)
- 200+ Ohio Revised Code traffic laws (driving)
- 30+ Columbus Municipal Code provisions (local traffic)
- 25+ Manual on Uniform Traffic Control Devices standards (signs/signals)
- 15+ Insurance requirements and regulations
- 10+ License and registration requirements

Approximately 395 regulatory touchpoints in 20 minutes of driving.

That's over 19 regulations per minute.

7:00 AM - AT WORK

John arrives at the building where he works. He clocks in, walks to his station, and begins his shift. For the next 8.5 hours, he will work under more regulations than he can count.

The Building Itself

The building John enters is subject to approximately 15,000 different regulations: the same Building Code, National Electrical Code, Plumbing Code, Fire Code, Mechanical Code, Energy Conservation Code, and ADA accessibility requirements that govern his house. Plus, additional OSHA workplace safety regulations.

The Workplace

John sits at his workstation. This desk, this chair, this computer are all regulated.

Occupational Safety and Health Administration (OSHA):

- General Duty Clause (employer must provide safe workplace)
- Hazard Communication Standard (chemical safety)
- Personal Protective Equipment standards (if required)
- Walking-Working Surfaces (slip/trip/fall prevention)
- Powered Industrial Trucks (forklift certification and operation)
- Electrical Safety (wiring, outlets, equipment)
- Emergency Action Plans (evacuation procedures)
- Fire Prevention Plans
- Bloodborne Pathogens Standard (first aid kits, exposure plans)

- Lockout/Tagout (machinery safety)

Employment Regulations: John's very presence at work is governed by:

- Fair Labor Standards Act (FLSA) - minimum wage, overtime, recordkeeping
- Title VII Civil Rights Act - discrimination prohibitions
- Americans with Disabilities Act (ADA) - accommodation requirements
- Age Discrimination in Employment Act (ADEA)
- Pregnancy Discrimination Act
- Equal Pay Act
- Family and Medical Leave Act (FMLA)
- National Labor Relations Act (unionization rights)
- Workers' Compensation requirements
- Unemployment insurance requirements
- Social Security withholding
- Medicare withholding
- Federal income tax withholding
- State income tax withholding
- Form I-9 employment eligibility verification
- E-Verify (in some states)

John didn't negotiate these terms. He didn't choose these protections. They were mandated before he ever applied for the job. The employer must comply or face penalties, fines, or closure.

The Work Itself

John's job is to manage inventory in a warehouse. Even this straightforward task is regulated.

- OSHA material handling standards (lifting, carrying, stacking)

- Warehouse racking regulations (load limits, inspection requirements)
- Forklift operation (certification required, OSHA training)
- Hazardous materials handling (if applicable)
- Inventory tracking systems (tax compliance, audit requirements)
- Data privacy regulations (customer information protection)
- Computer use policies (mandated by the company, often driven by regulations)
- Break requirements (Ohio law: no specific meal break required for adults, but breaks given must follow federal standards)
- Overtime regulations (time and a half after 40 hours per week)
- Record keeping (employer must track hours, wages, deductions)

Every movement John makes at work is observed, measured, and regulated. How he lifts a box. How he operates equipment. How he records data. How long he works. How much he's paid.

His employer doesn't set these rules out of kindness. The employer complies because non-compliance brings OSHA inspections, Department of Labor audits, discrimination lawsuits, workers' compensation claims, and potential criminal charges.

The Count at Work

In 8.5 hours at work, John is subject to approximately:

- 15,000+ building and safety codes (structure, fire, accessibility)
- 150+ OSHA workplace safety regulations
- 50+ employment law requirements (wage, hour, discrimination, benefits)
- 30+ material handling and job-specific regulations

Approximately 15,230 regulatory touchpoints during his workday. And the beautiful deception? John thinks his employer chose to hire him. John thinks he chose to work here. John thinks this is a voluntary arrangement.

But it's not. The employer must comply with 15,230+ regulations to even be allowed to hire John. John must submit to background checks, provide documentation, sign forms, agree to policies, and comply with workplace rules, or he cannot work.

This isn't employment. This is regulated participation in a system that controls every aspect of the relationship between employer and employee.

John is not free to negotiate his terms. The terms were set before he arrived. By the state. By the federal government. By regulatory agencies he's never heard of. By bureaucrats he's never met.

He's permitted to work. Not free to work. Permitted. And only if he complies.

And at 4:45 PM, when John drives home, he will face every single one of these regulations again. The same signs. The same laws. The same enforcement. The commute home is not freedom, it's a second submission to the same control.

But tonight, John needs to stop at Kroger. Sarah texted him a short list: milk, bread, eggs, chicken. A ten-minute stop that subjects him to another 500+ regulations he'll never see.

The health department inspections that control food storage temperatures. The FDA labeling requirements on every package. The USDA standards for the chicken he'll buy. The fire codes. The ADA compliance. The sanitation rules. The weights and measures laws ensuring the scale is accurate.

John walks in, grabs his items, pays, and leaves. Ten minutes. 500+ invisible regulations governing every product he touched, every transaction he made, every square foot he walked through.

This is not safety. This is control.

Every mile John drives, every turn he makes, every speed he maintains is dictated by someone else's rules. He is not free to drive as he sees fit. He is permitted to operate his vehicle only within the narrow parameters the state allows.

And if he steps outside those parameters by even a small margin, 10 mph over the limit, 3 feet too close to another car, one wheel over the white line, the state will take money from him through fines or increase his insurance rates through points on his record.

The road is not a path to work. The road is a regulated corridor where John's compliance is monitored, measured, and punished when fault can be found.

5:30 PM - HOME

John arrives home. He grills chicken on his back deck for dinner. The grill is subject to:

- Consumer Product Safety Commission standards
- UL safety certification
- Propane regulations (if gas grill)
- Local fire code (distance from structures)
- HOA rules (in some cases, what type of grill you can have)

The chicken is subject to:

- USDA poultry inspection
- Safe handling requirements
- Temperature requirements (must cook to 165°F)
- Storage requirements
- Expiration date regulations

John's back deck itself is subject to building code requirements: railing height and spacing, structural capacity, permits, setback requirements, and HOA approval.

10:30 PM - JOHN GOES TO SLEEP

John sets his alarm and goes to sleep. His mattress is subject to:

- 16 CFR Part 1633 - Flammability standard
- Labeling requirements
- Lead content restrictions
- Phthalate restrictions
- Formaldehyde limits

Even sleep is regulated.

THE COUNT: ONE DAY OF LAWS

Let me add this up. In a single day, from waking to sleeping, John was subject to approximately:

- Morning routine: 45 regulations
- House: 15,000+ regulations (structural, ongoing)
- Car: 100 regulations (vehicle standards)
- Commute: 200 traffic laws
- Workplace building: 15,000+ regulations
- Workplace safety (OSHA): 150+ regulations
- Employment: 50+ regulations
- Job-specific regulations: 30+
- Grocery store: 500+ regulations (on the store and products)
- Evening at home: 50+ regulations

Conservative estimate: John's single day involved approximately 31,125 regulatory touchpoints.

That's 31,125 laws controlling every aspect of his day, from the building he works in to the food he buys

And this is just one day. This is just what's visible. This doesn't include:

- The thousands of regulations governing the infrastructure he uses (roads, power grid, water system, internet)
- The financial regulations governing his bank accounts, credit cards, investments
- The educational regulations governing his children's school
- The healthcare regulations governing his insurance and medical care

And we haven't even mentioned the tax code.
Every dollar John earned today, every transaction he made, every deduction he might claim next April, all of it governed by **74,000 pages of federal tax law containing over 75,000 distinct provisions.** John has never read them. He can't. Tax attorneys can't master them. Even IRS agents give conflicting answers to the same tax questions.
Yet John is legally required to comply with all of it, perfectly, or face penalties, interest, liens, and imprisonment.
The system is so complex that **everyone is always in potential violation.** Which means the state has leverage over everyone, at any time, for any reason.
All of this isn't accidental.
If we counted every regulation that touches John's life (not just in his average day, but in the systems he's embedded in) the number would be in the hundreds of thousands.

THE COST OF DISOBEDIENCE
What happens if John breaks one of these rules?

- Rolling through a stop sign: $150 fine
- Speeding 10 mph over: $165 fine
- Parking violation: $45-$500 depending on violation
- Building code violation: $250-$5,000 per violation

- HOA violation: $50-$500 per violation
- OSHA violation: $7,000-$136,532 per violation (on employer)
- Food safety violation: $500-$10,000 per violation, possible closure
- Tax violation: penalties, interest, possible criminal charges
- Employment law violation: $10,000-$500,000+ in damages
- Environmental violation: $25,000-$50,000 per day

Every single rule is backed by force. Every single regulation has a punishment attached. If you step out of line enough, they will use fear to keep you under control. The fines not enough to paralyze you? No problem. The tyrant has built systems to take your freedom away entirely. Let's see if the threat of jail will keep you obedient.

You are not free. You are managed. You are controlled. You are governed in every moment of every day from the instant you wake until the moment you sleep.

This is not civilization. This is not order. This is not protection.

This is enslavement by a million paper cuts. Control so complete that you don't even see it. This is the tyrant's work: a prison made of rules, where every bar is invisible, but every bar is real.

And the deceit is calling this freedom.

LAWS THAT PROTECT GREED

You've seen the greed. You've seen how John paid $62,567 in total profit extracted for a car that cost $18,000 to manufacture. You've seen the 31,125 + laws that govern his every move from waking to sleeping.

Now let me show you how greed and the laws work together. How they coordinate. How they protect each other.

This is not an accident. This is not coincidence. This is the same darkness in industry and government that enslaves you.

THE LAW THAT FORCES YOU TO PAY THE MIDDLEMAN

Remember John's car? The dealership made a $4,744 profit just for being a middleman.

But if John had wanted to buy new, he couldn't have bought directly from Honda. The law won't allow it.

All 50 states have laws that prohibit car manufacturers from selling directly to consumers. You must buy from a dealership. This is the law.

Read that again. It is **illegal** in every single state for Honda to sell a car directly to John. The law **requires** a middleman. The law **mandates** that someone takes profit from the transaction without adding value to the car.

Why?

Because the dealerships lobbied for it.

The Lobbying Machine

The National Automobile Dealers Association (NADA) is one of the most powerful lobbying forces in America:

- 2024 lobbying spending: $5.49 million
- 2024 political contributions: $3.22 million

They don't just lobby Congress; they lobby every single state legislature By 2010, they had successfully passed laws in all 50 states prohibiting direct manufacturer sales.

These laws accomplish one thing: **mandate the middleman.**

They prohibit manufacturers from owning dealerships, require all new cars to be sold through franchised dealers, protect existing dealers from competition, and make it nearly impossible to terminate a dealer franchise.

The Cost to You

Economists have studied these laws:

A 1972 study found that franchise laws raised new car prices by 9%

Goldman Sachs estimated that direct manufacturer sales could save consumers $2,225 on a $26,000 car

A 2025 analyst report estimated direct sales would cut vehicle costs by 8.6%

Those studies measure *average* dealer markup, but miss the full chain of extraction.

John's car shows the reality: the regional distributor markup ($2,500) plus the dealership markup and fees ($7,500) equals $10,000 in middleman costs. That's 26% of the $38,500 sale price, three times higher than the "average" because it includes dealer fees, extended warranties, paint protection, and other profit centers that don't show up in the base markup statistics.

The studies measure what dealers report. John's receipt shows what consumers actually pay.

Multiply even the *conservative* estimate ($3,500 per car) by 15 million new cars sold annually: $52.5 billion taken from people's lives. And that's the low end.

Protected by law. Mandated by government.

The Tesla Fight Proves It Still Exists

In the 2010s, Tesla tried to sell cars directly to consumers online. **Every single state dealership association sued them.**

State by state, Tesla had to fight for the right to sell its own cars:

Texas, Virginia, Michigan: Banned Tesla direct sales

Louisiana enacted a law in 2017 explicitly banning direct sales to stop Tesla

As of 2025: 17 states explicitly ban direct sales; Tesla is banned or restricted in 28 states
And it's not just Tesla. In 2025:
Scout Motors (Volkswagen subsidiary) planned direct sales. NADA filed lawsuit (February 2025)
Sony Honda Mobility (Afeela brand) planned direct sales. The California New Car Dealers Association filed a lawsuit (August 2025)
The dealerships are still fighting. Still lobbying. Still protecting their government-mandated profits.

The Pattern: Greed protects greed, and uses law enforcement to protect its profits.

Do you see it now? Here's the cycle:

- **Industry makes profits** (dealerships extracting $4,744 from John)
- **Industry uses profits to lobby** (NADA spends $5.49 million per year)
- **Politicians pass laws** (all 50 states ban direct sales)
- **Laws protect industry profits** (consumers are forced to use dealerships)
- **Profits increase** (industry has more money to lobby)
- **Cycle repeats**

This is legal bribery. This is government-sponsored greed. The tyrant uses the force of law to take from your life.
It's Not Just Cars
This same pattern exists everywhere.
Insurance Laws: Most states mandate car insurance. You are required by law to buy a product from a private company. Insurance companies

are top political donors every cycle. Result: You must pay insurance companies, by law.

Certificate of Need Laws (Healthcare): 35 states require hospitals to get government permission before opening. Protects existing hospitals from competition. Heavily lobbied for by hospital associations. Result: Healthcare costs stay high; law blocks new competition.

Occupational Licensing Laws: Need a license to cut hair? To arrange flowers? To be an interior designer? These laws don't protect consumers; they protect existing businesses from competition. Heavily lobbied for by industry associations. Result: Fewer competitors, higher prices for you.

Pharmaceutical Patent Laws: 20-year monopolies on drugs. Heavily lobbied for by pharma companies (some of the biggest lobbyists in DC). Result: Americans pay 2-3 times more for prescription drugs than any other country.

Zoning Laws: Restrict what can be built, where, and how much. Lobbied for by existing property owners and developers. Result: Housing prices artificially inflated, supply restricted.

Do you see the pattern?

Industry funds lobbyists. Lobbyists buy politicians. Politicians write laws. Laws protect profits. Profits fund more lobbyists. More lobbyists buy more laws. More laws to enslave you.

The Beautiful Lie

The lie they tell you is: "These laws protect you. Dealerships provide a valuable service. Licensing ensures quality. Regulations keep you safe."

The truth: These laws protect profits. They ensure you have no choice but to pay middlemen. They guarantee that politically connected industries extract wealth from you by force of law.

This is not capitalism. Capitalism is voluntary exchange. This is **government sponsored theft**, where government and industry collude to force you to pay.

This is not a free market. Free markets allow competition. This is a **captured market**, where laws prevent competition to protect greed.

This is not civilization. Civilization is voluntary cooperation. This is systematic greed, backed by the force of law, enforced by the state, designed to steal maximum wealth from your labor while calling it "freedom."

The greed you saw in the car's first purchase wasn't random. It was protected by law. Mandated by law. Enforced by law.

The 31,125 regulations governing John's day aren't about safety. Many of them exist to protect business interests from competition.

The tyrant doesn't just take from you directly. The tyrant creates a system where private businesses take from you, and the government makes it illegal for you to escape.

This is the coordination. This is the collusion. This is the trap.

Greed works through government to enslave you.

THE PATTERN REVEALED

Look at all these laws. Look at all these regulations. Look at how they work together.

Who benefits?

- **The government collects the fines.**
- **The government employs the enforcers.**
- **The government justifies its existence through the complexity it creates.**

But it's not just government greed. It's deeper than that.

The dealerships lobby for laws forcing you to use dealerships. The insurance companies lobby for laws forcing you to buy insurance. The hospitals lobby for laws blocking competing hospitals. Every industry with political power lobbies for laws that protect their profits.

And the government? The government gets paid at every single point of contact.

First, they get paid by the industries:

- Campaign contributions
- "Speaking fees" (bribes with a respectable name)
- Donations to their foundations
- Promises of cushy jobs after they leave office (the "revolving door")
- Lobbying money to influence legislation

Second, they get paid by you through taxes:

- Federal income tax (21% of John's gross income)
- State income tax (7.2% of John's gross income)
- Social Security tax (taken before you see a dollar)
- Medicare tax (taken before you see a dollar)
- Property tax (pay yearly or they take your house)
- Sales tax (every purchase you make)
- Gas tax (federal and state, every gallon)
- Unemployment insurance tax (your employer pays, but it's part of your compensation you never see)

Third, they get paid through fees:

- Vehicle registration ($122/year in Ohio)
- Driver's license renewal
- Title transfer fees

- Plate fees
- Building permits (want to renovate your house? Pay the government first)
- Business licenses
- Professional licenses
- Fishing licenses (charging to catch what God provides)
- Inspection fees
- Court filing fees
- Passport fees
- Marriage license fees
- Birth certificate fees
- Death certificate fees (they charge you to prove you died)

Fourth, they get paid through fines:

- Traffic tickets ($150 for rolling a stop sign)
- Parking violations
- Building code violations ($250-$5,000 per violation)
- HOA violations (often enforced through city ordinances)
- Late payment penalties on taxes
- Environmental violations
- Zoning violations
- Business regulation violations

Fifth, they get paid through mandates that force you to buy from private companies:

- Mandatory car insurance (private companies profit, government enforces the mandate)
- Mandatory health insurance (Affordable Care Act individual mandate, though penalty removed)
- Certificate requirements that force you to hire licensed contractors

- Inspection requirements that force you to pay inspection companies

Every single interaction with the government comes with a price tag.
You can't drive without paying them. You can't own a house without paying them. You can't work without paying them. You can't buy without paying them. **You can't even die without paying them.**

And if you refuse to pay? They fine you. If you refuse to pay the fine? They take your property. If you refuse to let them take your property? They send men with guns to take it from you.

Every regulation requires enforcement. Every enforcer requires payment. Every payment comes from you.
The system is self-sustaining. The tyrant creates rules that require enforcement that requires payment that requires your labor that requires you to obey the rules.

This is the prison. This is the chain. This is the enslavement.

And the beautiful lie whispered every day: "These rules keep you safe. These laws protect you. This is freedom with responsibility."
No. This is enslavement by deceit.
You are not free. You have never been free. Every moment of your life is regulated, monitored, controlled, and taxed.

THE TRUTH YOU NEED TO SEE
This didn't happen by accident. This level of coordination, this systematic enslavement across every aspect of human life, across every industry, across every level of government, across every nation on Earth...

This cannot be explained by calling it human greed alone. Yes, humans manifest greed. Yes, businesses are run by humans. Yes, politicians are human.

But this? This level of systematic coordination? Across centuries? Across continents? Affecting billions of people in exactly the same patterns?

No man could coordinate this. No group of men could maintain this. No conspiracy of humans could create a system this comprehensive, this invisible, this effective at enslaving the entire human race. And nearly no one sees it?

The tyrant has infected every level of human existence. He has built a prison so sophisticated that the prisoners defend it. He has created chains so invisible that the slaves think it is of their own doing. Pride whispers...you did it.

Can you see it yet?

Every stop sign is a rule you must obey or pay. Every speed limit is a control you must follow or face punishment. Every regulation is a restriction on your choices. Every law is a chain. Every lobbied law is greed using government force to take from you.

This is your life. This is everyone's life.

And the ones who have mastered this life? The life of deceit and greed? Pride fills their hearts. But what have they won? They've mastered the system of darkness. Is he who plays by darkness's rules and succeeds filled with light? No, he is a part of the darkness himself.

"Do not love the world or anything in the world. If anyone loves the world, love for the Father is not in them." (1 John 2:15, NIV)

THE TYRANT

This is the world the tyrant has infected. Those who succeed in it believe they've won. But there is no winning here. You can only choose whose side you're on. You wake up every day and walk into it, believing you are free because you chose which cage to occupy, which chain to wear, which master to serve.

But God did not create this.

God created freedom. God created abundance. God created a world where you were meant to live without these chains.

Something infected the creation.

Something contaminated the minds that built these regulations. Something planted greed in every living thing. Something enslaved the creation and called it freedom. Something wove this web through every government, every nation, every age of human history.
This is a darkness manifesting in economic and legal structures. This is what Paul warned about in Ephesians 6:12. The battle isn't what it appears to be. It isn't against the people you see. It works through systems. Through industries. Through governments. Through laws. Through you..

"For our struggle is not against flesh and blood"

You're not fighting car dealerships. You're not fighting insurance companies. You're not fighting politicians.

You're fighting the spiritual force that coordinates all of them.
You are fighting the tyrant: Satan himself.

And now you know. Now you see.

The question is: what will you do with this knowledge?

You may be thinking: "This is overwhelming. This is too big. This has been going on forever. What can one person do against a system this entrenched?" And you're right about one thing: this is not new. But that doesn't mean you're powerless.

NOTHING NEW UNDER THE SUN

Is there anything new under the sun?

Yes. You.

Although this has been going on for thousands of years, you have not been around for thousands of years. So each new birth allows for a new deceit. To make you believe that this is a normal life, and this is what you should do. And to make you focus on this world, forgetting the spiritual life you were meant to shape here.

It enslaves you so fiercely that you do not pay attention to your spiritual life. Because you are so busy trying to keep your head above water that you forget (or you don't even see) the reason that you're here.

You're not here to work 25 days a month to enrich other people. You're not here to give your life to others out of obligatory enslavement. Going out on that boat four days a week isn't your goal. Feeding greed isn't why you're here, nor to let hate take from you. These distractions are meant and designed intentionally to keep you from looking at what is important: **Your life.**

Your life is everything. Your spirit holds the possibility of an eternal future of incredible love and sharing. But you'll never see that possibility if you believe this world's greatest lie: that everything you need is here, that everything you are is flesh, that what you see and touch is all there is.

This is the deception that leads to your destruction.

But there is hope.
To find it, you must first understand what this world truly offers.

PART FOUR: THE SPIRITUAL BATTLE

You've seen the prison. You've counted the bars; thousands of regulations controlling your every move in just one day. You've traced the greed, every hand in your pocket, every system designed to take from your life. You understand the coordination, government and industry working together to keep you enslaved.

But all of this, the debt, the laws, the fees, the fines, the regulations, these are just symptoms. These are the visible manifestations of something you cannot see with your eyes.
The enslavement you experience through your wallet, in your schedule, in your stress is not the root problem.

It's the fruit of it. The root is spiritual.

The system that enslaves you was built by contaminated minds, influenced by contaminated thoughts, listening to whispers of pride, hate, greed, selfishness, lust and more.
This is not a human conspiracy. What man could live long enough to enslave every generation? What organization could infiltrate every nation? What human mind could replicate the same deception across thousands of years in cultures that never met? This requires something beyond man.

This is spiritual warfare. And you are the battlefield.

"For our struggle is not against flesh and blood, but against the rulers, against the authorities, against the powers of this dark world and against the spiritual forces of evil in the heavenly realms." (Ephesians 6:12, NIV)

Your struggle is not against your boss. Not against the bank. Not against the government. Not against any human institution or person. Your struggle is against the spiritual forces behind them. The tyrant who contaminates all of this. Satan himself.

Watch how this works in the world you can see. It starts with a single choice. The same choice Adam faced. The same choice you face every day.

The Garden Overtaken by Weeds

You must recognize this place for what it is: a garden that has been taken over by weeds. The weeds can either choke you out and destroy your life, or you can stand against them and claim the gift that has been offered to you. You must see through all of this darkness and through all of this enslavement. You must know there is light, a hope beyond this place.

This is just a temporary garden. A place where the fruit of your spirit can be picked, and you can go on to live eternal life in a place God created without all of this enslavement. You are seeing a training ground designed to sharpen you, a base of resistance against darkness itself.

So the question becomes:

-Do you fall to the resistance or do you stand against it?

-Do you forge ahead no matter the darkness that stands against you?

-Do you choose love when you're surrounded by hate?

-Do you choose to give when greed pulls you down?

-Do you choose to walk through the darkness to find the light?

This enslavement, the darkness that continually threatens your life here on earth, has no power over the spirit if you choose the light. But this choice isn't in your thoughts, because we know our thoughts are contaminated. This choice is through action. I don't choose God; I don't choose life, by merely thinking about the choice. That is not enough. You must act against the darkness and try with everything in you not to fall prey to it.

When hate is near you, and the fear within you wants to paralyze you, you must act. When the greed within yourself says save everything and don't give a penny away, you must act. When pride says everything is yours, you earned it, you must act against this immediately.

You must physically act and walk toward love, kindness and giving, to combat all the forces that stand against you.

No, this is not an easy task. It is extremely difficult. But heaven belongs only to the ones who fight for life. There is no coasting across the finish line and getting the greatest prize that has ever been created. You do not get to mention God occasionally or say that God is love and inherit God's kingdom.

That holy kingdom, that is so precious, and so valuable, is only for those who actively choose, who choose to give their life, who choose to give their possessions, who choose to give their love, who choose to give kindness.

The Deception

"Not everyone who says to me, 'Lord, Lord,' will enter the kingdom of heaven, but only the one who does the will of my Father who is in heaven. Many will say to me on that day, 'Lord, Lord, did we not prophesy in your name and in your name drive out demons and in your name perform many miracles?' Then I will tell them plainly, 'I never knew you. Away from me, you evildoers!'" (Matthew 7:21-23, NIV)

Have you ever wondered what that verse meant? How could someone do miracles in God's name and not even be known by Him? It is because of the deception of the mind. Satan makes us believe we serve God when we don't. That's a horrific thought, isn't it? You may believe you're following God, and you are not.

Christians who solely serve the church are not serving God. They are hiding from the darkness. Jesus said:

"Neither do people light a lamp and put it under a bowl. Instead they put it on its stand, and it gives light to everyone in the house. In the same way, let your light shine before others, that they may see your good deeds and glorify your Father in heaven." (Matthew 5:15-16, NIV)

Do you understand what Jesus is saying?
A lamp gives light to a dark house. Not to other lamps.

If you have light within you and you only serve inside the church, you are hiding your light among other lights. The church doesn't need your light; it already has light. The darkness outside needs your light.

This is one of Satan's most effective strategies within the church: keep believers comfortable inside, serving each other, never venturing into the darkness where light is actually needed. If he can trap your light in the light, the darkness remains unthreatened.

And on judgment day, many will point to their church activity as proof:

"But Lord, I did great miracles in your name."

God can work through anyone. He enabled Balaam's donkey to speak. Was that a miracle? Yes. It was a talking donkey! Did the donkey take credit? Did the donkey say, "Look what I did in the Lord's name"?

Do you think that because God worked miracles through you, you'll have a seat in heaven next to the talking donkey? Because if miracles guarantee salvation, that donkey has a better claim than most Christians.

God does the miracles. You don't. And being used by God doesn't mean you're saved by God.

Only those who chose God and fought with everything within them for life, only those who chose light in the darkness, only those who finished the race, inherit the kingdom of God.

The Thief on the Cross: Understanding True Salvation

The story of Jesus on the cross with the two thieves is known by most:

"One of the criminals who hung there hurled insults at him: 'Aren't you the Messiah? Save yourself and us!' But the other criminal rebuked him. 'Don't you fear God,' he said, 'since you are under the same sentence? We are punished justly, for we are getting what our deeds deserve. But this man has done nothing wrong.' Then he said, 'Jesus, remember me when you come into your kingdom.' Jesus answered him, 'Truly I tell you, today you will be with me in paradise.'" (Luke 23:39-43, NIV)

The story is often used to show that you don't enter heaven through works.

The deceit you believe as truth:

All you have to do is say the name of God, believe that God exists, and you can enter heaven easily.

Is this true?

Maybe.

It depends on the timing of your death.

The truth of this story is this:
You see, this man chose God moments before his death.

He didn't have time to turn back to sin.
He didn't have time to go choose greed again and again.
He didn't have time to let pride take over and say, "All of this is mine," or, "I did this."
This man on the cross **didn't have time** to let lust come in and desire things of the world.

This is what many have failed to see in the story. Satan didn't get another chance to contaminate the thief's spirit. God saved the man in that moment, and he was gone minutes later.

If you choose God, you are saved. Let me repeat that: if you choose God, you are saved. But fail to choose God enough times and the spirit becomes contaminated again, while the mind believes it is saved.

This is the great deceit of Satan. "Once saved, always saved." Fall for this lie, and you will pay with your life. This is critical to understand.

"Lord, Lord, I did many great things in your name." "Get away from me for I do not know you."

This is how this happens. In your mind, you believe you have chosen God, and you live for Him. But your spirit has been slowly contaminated without you knowing it.

You slowly chose pride over time. Greed became your master again. Selfishness became your good friend. Hate crept in where love once was. Satan does not stop attacking. The demons never stop. 24 hours a day, seven days a week, they are working fiercely to contaminate your spirit.

They do not rest, and neither should you. You have to fight their continuous contamination.

You have to choose love constantly.

You have to give constantly.

You have to seek God constantly.

Every moment of every day you have to choose God, or the darkness will slowly creep in. Your mind will believe you are saved, but your spirit will become too contaminated to save. This is what darkness does and you're not even aware of it.

Soon the darkness feels more comfortable to you than the light. This happens because the demons within you have contaminated the spirit. That's why you can be around people who gossip (which is hate) with no issues. You can become good friends with people who are greedy, and it doesn't bother you. You begin to think these are normal behaviors because you hear the same whispers inside of you. This is the danger.

When hate begins to feel normal, hate has won. When being greedy instead of generous is your go-to choice, greed has won. When lust after the things of this world wins you over, lust has won. When you feel good about what you have accomplished, pride has won.

These are indicators that your spirit has been contaminated.

The Cost of Inheritance
Here's what the churches don't teach: to inherit the kingdom of God, someone must die.

Yes, Jesus died. His death paid the price for sin. His sacrifice opened the way. But there's another death required, one that no one talks about because it costs everything.

You must die.

Not a physical death, though that will come. You must die to this world. Pride must die. Greed must die. Fear must die. Lust must die. Hate must die. Selfishness must die. All the darkness clinging to your spirit must die.

"Very truly I tell you, unless a kernel of wheat falls to the ground and dies, it remains only a single seed. But if it dies, it produces many seeds. Anyone who loves their life will lose it, while anyone who hates their life in this world will keep it for eternal life." (John 12:24-25, NIV)

"I have been crucified with Christ and I no longer live, but Christ lives in me. The life I now live in the body, I live by faith in the Son of God, who loved me and gave himself for me." (Galatians 2:20, NIV)

To inherit the kingdom, you must die to everything this world tells you to cling to. This is the truth hidden in plain sight throughout Scripture. This is the cost few are willing to pay.

But what does this actually look like?
How does the spiritual battle play out in your daily choices?

What Daily Choices Reveal
Every day, you make thousands of choices. Most seem insignificant. But every choice reveals which master you serve.
Ask yourself honestly:

-What causes you to negotiate a selling or buying price with someone?
-What causes you to look at other people and compare yourself to them?
-What causes you to talk about people when they are not present?
-What causes you to take your foot off the accelerator when you see a cop working radar?
-What causes you to want a bigger house or a newer car?
-What causes you to respond angrily to someone?
-What causes you to want to please the people around you?
-What causes you to avoid conflict?

I can illuminate the darkness and its traits, but you have to look inside your own life and see how you respond to these questions. The truth is, there is a spiritual force influencing your responses to these questions, a force that is not you. But when you choose to act on those influences, you become the owner of that decision. You become responsible for the actions you take.

You see, darkness just influences you, but you have a choice. Do I take road A or do I take road B? In the end, you cannot blame the darkness and say, 'It made me do it.' God has given you the strength to stand up against the influence of darkness and to choose what is good. You don't get to point the finger at Satan. The choice is yours.

But being aware of the darkness influencing your life can help you choose good instead. Because whether or not you see it, the vast majority of your normal decisions lead you toward darkness. Only the smallest percentage leads you toward good.

"Enter through the narrow gate. For wide is the gate and broad is the road that leads to destruction, and many enter through it. But small is the gate and narrow the road that leads to life, and only a few find it." (Matthew 7:13-14, NIV)

The truth is, the easy road feels right. What feels natural to the flesh is darkness influencing your life. This is why you cannot trust your feelings, they deceive you.

Nowhere in the Bible does it say: "Trust your feelings, for they will guide you to the correct path."

This is why you have to choose God at every moment of your day. You must know His Word because it is the guide that keeps you on the path towards the light. Yes, you live in enslavement while you're in the flesh, and yes, your entire life here will be influenced by evil. But this is not the issue. This is not the problem.

Because the darkness is what refines you.

The pressures of the darkness all around you create a spirit so beautiful and so pristine from the refinement it offers. Extreme pressures create diamonds, and your spirit develops under the extreme pressures of this life.

God is creating a good so pure in you that it could not have been obtained without the pressure of darkness. God takes what is evil, what causes suffering, and He turns it into something so beautiful and so amazing that the human mind cannot even comprehend it.

This is the reason God gives us simple instructions on how to follow the light. How we should follow Him until the end of this race. You must run this race with everything you have in you. You must stand against the influence of darkness that wants to influence your steps and say: no.

Your actions must shout out:
I stand for God!
I stand for what's right!
I stand for love!

THE TYRANT

I stand for life!

But see how subtle the battle is. See how darkness disguises itself as harmless pleasure, as entertainment, as escape. Consider how this spiritual battle appears in something as simple as entertainment, how evil fuels evil to create an entire industry.

The Slot Machine

Margaret is 68 years old. She lives alone in a small apartment in Arizona. Every month, she tucks a little money away into an envelope she keeps in her kitchen drawer. She calls it her "Vegas fund."

Twice a year, she takes a bus to Las Vegas. She stays at the same casino hotel she's been going to for twelve years now, ever since her husband died. It's become her ritual. Her escape.

Margaret sits at her favorite slot machine. She likes this one because the seat is comfortable and it's near the bathrooms. For hours at a time, she feeds bills into the machine. She pulls the lever. The numbers scroll. The lights flash. Sometimes bells ring. Sometimes nothing. She keeps pulling.

The waitress knows her name. Brings her free drinks. Margaret feels seen. Feels important. Feels alive. The machine gives her hope. Maybe this pull will be the big one. Maybe this is when everything changes.

Margaret tells her friends back home about the times she wins. She doesn't talk about the envelope in her kitchen drawer that never seems to have enough in it anymore. She doesn't mention that she's been going twice a year for twelve years and has nothing to show for it except depressing memories of losing all of her savings.

Entire industries flourish on this model. Can you see what's really happening spiritually?

This is hate feeding greed. Greed enslaves you through the machine. Hate destroys you through the enslavement. But you allow it because of the greed within you. The greed that wants its chance at pleasure. The greed that believes the next pull will be different. This is what the demons do to us.

Margaret doesn't see what's influencing her. She doesn't understand the thoughts whispering that the next pull will be different are not hers. This feels "good" to her. Why? Because it's the pleasure that darkness derives from destroying a life.

Pull after pull, she's choosing greed. Her spirit darkens. Not all at once. Slowly. The envelope in her kitchen drawer gets lighter. The bills get harder to pay. The darkness deepens. The pleasure she feels at the machine is the very thing destroying her.

She's being consumed from within.

This is the model of the world. This is how darkness operates. It promises you pleasure, it promises you escape, it promises you freedom, and it takes everything.

This is not just Margaret's story. This is just one example in one person. This is the model everywhere.

But survival isn't about avoiding the darkness. It's about finishing in spite of it.

Finishing the Race

In the mountains of Tennessee, there's a race called the Barkley Marathons. It's not on roads. There are no aid stations. No cheering crowds. Just 100 miles of brutal wilderness, unmarked trails, and a 60-hour time limit.

THE TYRANT

Only about 40 runners are allowed to attempt it each year after grueling entrance requirements. Since 1986, only 20 people have finished out of over 1,000 who've tried.

The Barkley doesn't care how fast you start. It doesn't care about your resume or your early pace.

It only cares if you finish.

Every year, elite athletes line up at the starting gate. Strong. Prepared. Confident. Some lead for miles. Some dominate the early loops. But the Barkley strips away illusions. Navigation fails. Fatigue sets in. And one by one, runners who looked unstoppable, fail to complete the course.

At the Barkley, your first twenty miles mean nothing. In fact, nobody remembers the names of those who started the race, but the finishers are well known.

The Barkley measures endurance in miles and hours. But Scripture tells the same story with eternal stakes, except the course is your lifetime, and the finish line is death of the flesh.

Solomon started strong. He loved the Lord. When God offered him anything, Solomon asked for wisdom instead of wealth. And God gave him more wisdom than any human before or since. Solomon wrote Proverbs, Ecclesiastes, Song of Songs. His insight shaped nations. By every early metric, Solomon looked like he couldn't lose.

But Solomon didn't finish.

"As Solomon grew old, his wives turned his heart after other gods, and his heart was not fully devoted to the Lord his God, as the heart of David his father had been." (1 Kings 11:4, NIV)

"He had seven hundred wives of royal birth and three hundred concubines, and his wives led him astray." (1 Kings 11:3, NIV)

And when God told Solomon that the kingdom would be torn from him and given to his servant, Solomon's response wasn't repentance. **It was murder.** He tried to kill Jeroboam, the man God had chosen to succeed him (1 Kings 11:40). Solomon didn't just drift into compromise, **he actively fought against God's will.**

Solomon built high places for idol worship in Israel. The man who built God's temple ended his race building altars to false gods. Pleasure replaced obedience, pride replaced humility, and foolishness replaced wisdom. His spirit became contaminated. And Scripture records his failure with brutal honesty.

Solomon's life confronts a truth we resist: starting strong doesn't guarantee we finish the race. Writing Scripture, building temples, offering sacrifices: none of these substitute for salvation in the end.

This is why Paul's final words carry weight:

"I have fought the good fight, I have finished the race, I have kept the faith." (2 Timothy 4:7, NIV)

Paul doesn't list churches planted. He doesn't point to miracles or influence. He points to completion.

He finished.

THE TYRANT

The Barkley exposes this truth in the flesh: good intentions without perseverance don't reach the end. Solomon's life shows us: wisdom without obedience leads to ruin. And Paul shows us what matters: not how brilliantly the race begins, but whether faith remains when the course grows lonely, confusing, and costly.

The tyrant doesn't care about your strong start. He only cares that you don't finish. He wants compromise, corruption, and collapse, just like Solomon.

But God doesn't measure your race by the first mile. He measures it by the last.

Satan is counting on you to quit.
God is counting on you to finish.

The question isn't whether you can run. The question is whether you'll endure when the path gets dark, when your strength fails, when every voice tells you to stop.

Will you finish?

PART FIVE: THE TRUTH ABOUT SLAVERY

God's People Under Bondage

You are enslaved. Your kids are following in the same footsteps. You work to pay interest to banks. You obey regulations you never agreed to. You surrender your time, your money, your freedom to a system designed to extract everything from you. You've seen John's life. You've felt the weight. Now you need to see the spiritual truth behind it all: what you're living under is not just economic slavery, it's something far older, far deeper, and far more complete.

So, what are you to do now?

You live in a condemned world, a slave to the darkness of your own flesh. First, you must see it. Because if you remain blind, you remain a slave, powerless.

"Jesus replied, 'Very truly I tell you, everyone who sins is a slave to sin. Now a slave has no permanent place in the family, but a son belongs to it forever. So if the Son sets you free, you will be free indeed.'" (John 8:34-36, NIV)

"Don't you know that when you offer yourselves to someone as obedient slaves, you are slaves of the one you obey, whether you are slaves to sin, which leads to death, or to obedience, which leads to righteousness?" (Romans 6:16, NIV)

Know that what I'm saying isn't anything new. This has been happening for thousands of years. So what is different about what you're reading? It's about being conscious of the spiritual darkness that has enslaved you. This ultimately will only resonate with the people who have questioned this life here on earth, our existence and our purpose.

The Architecture of Modern Slavery

The slavery you live under is more complete than anything that came before it. The plantation owners of the 1800s could only enslave the body. They could force labor, they could restrict movement, and they could control physical actions. But the mind? The mind could remain free. The spirit could resist. Hope could survive.

Spiritual slavery is far more complete. It enslaves the body through debt. It enslaves the mind through education and media. It enslaves the spirit with contaminated thought itself. And most devastatingly, it makes you believe freedom is slavery and slavery is freedom.

The system is by design. The government creates the framework. The corporations fill in the details. The bank provides the chains. And you, you wake up every morning, check your phone, drink your coffee, and walk directly into the cage, believing you're free because you chose which cage to enter.

But you didn't choose. The choice was made for you long before you were born. You were born into a system that had already decided your value, your purpose, your limitations.

The Illusion of Choice

Let's examine John's life again, but this time through the lens of choice.

Education:

When John was 5 years old, did anyone ask him if he wanted to go to school? No, the state mandated it. He had to go, or his parents faced legal consequences.

When John was 18, did anyone present him with real alternatives to college? No. Every authority figure in his life (parents, teachers, guidance counselors, society) told him the same thing: "You need a degree to succeed. You need a degree to get a good job. You need a degree to have a future."

The alternative? Poverty. Minimum wage. Being looked down upon. Being considered a failure.

So John "chose" college. He took on $40,000 in student loan debt at 18 years old, an age when he couldn't legally drink alcohol because society deemed him too immature to make that decision, but mature enough to sign documents that would enslave him financially for the next 20 years.

Did John choose this? Or was the choice made for him by a system that had already decided: "You will go to college, you will take on debt, and you will spend your adult life paying for the privilege of entering our workforce."

Employment:

After college, John "chose" his career. But did he really?

He needed money to pay his student loans. He needed health insurance (mandated by law at the time, and practically mandatory regardless because medical bankruptcy is the leading cause of bankruptcy in America). He needed a steady income to qualify for an apartment, a car loan, and a credit card.

So, John applied for jobs. Not jobs he was passionate about. Not jobs that fulfilled his purpose. But jobs that paid enough to service his debt and provide the benefits he was required to have.

He interviewed. He accepted an offer. He signed the employment contract.

The world calls this "choice." But when every option leads to the same cage, is it really a choice?

John didn't choose to need a degree. The system chose that for him.

Housing:

John got married. He and Sarah decided they needed a house. Why? Because that's what you're supposed to do. That's "the American Dream." That's "building wealth." That's "stability."

But let's examine this choice:

Option 1: Rent. Pay $1,500/month for an apartment. Build zero equity. Enrich a landlord. Be subject to rent increases. Risk eviction. Have no control over your living space.

Option 2: Buy. Take on $300,000+ in debt. Pay the bank $2,400/month (more than rent) for 30 years. Pay $500,000+ total for a house worth $300,000. Build equity (but only after 10+ years of payments going mostly to interest). Risk foreclosure if you miss payments. Pay property taxes forever (because you never truly own property. You just pay the government for the right to live on it) or lose the house even after paying it off.

These are your choices. Rent and own nothing, or buy and owe everything.

John "chose" to buy. But what he really chose was which form of enslavement he preferred.

The system had already decided: You will not own property outright. You will not live without paying someone for shelter. You will work to enrich either a landlord or a bank. The choice of which master to serve is yours.

And the deceit? "This is freedom."

Transportation:

John needs a car. Why? Because American cities are designed around car ownership. Public transportation is deliberately under-funded and inefficient in most places. Jobs are not within walking distance of affordable housing. Groceries are not accessible without a vehicle.

The system decided: You will need a car.

THE TYRANT

So John's "choice" is:
What kind of car? New or used? Financed or leased? Honda or Toyota? But the fundamental question (Do I need a car at all?) was answered before John was born. The infrastructure was built. The cities were designed. The public transportation was defunded. John's choice was taken away by decisions made 50-70 years ago.

John didn't choose to need a car. The system chose that for him. John only chose which chain to wear: the chain of a Honda or the chain of a Toyota.

The Pattern Repeats

Look at every major "choice" in John's life:

Health insurance: Required by law (until recently) and practically mandatory, regardless. John's choice: which insurance company extracts money from him.

Cell phone: Try getting a job without a phone number. Try staying connected to family without one. Try navigating without GPS. Fear of not being able to contact someone in an emergency. John's choice: which carrier enslaves him.

Internet: Required for most jobs now (work from home, emails, applications). Required for children's education. Required for basic tasks like paying bills or accessing government services. John's choice: which ISP charges him $80/month.

Food: John must eat. But grocery stores are designed to maximize the money they take. Healthy food costs more. Processed food is subsidized and cheap. Fast food companies engineer food to be addictive. John's choice: which form of nutritional enslavement he prefers.

Retirement: Social Security won't be enough (by design). John must save in a 401(k) (pretax, so he pays taxes later when he withdraws, and if he withdraws early, penalties). The stock market (which could crash at any time; see 2008, 2020). John's choice: which financial institution manages his enslavement to future uncertainty.

Every "choice" John makes is a choice between chains. Chrome chains or steel chains. Leather chains, or rope chains. But chains nonetheless.

The Slave Who Defends His Master

Here's the most treacherous part of modern slavery: the slaves defend it.

Suggest to John that the system is designed to enslave him, and what will he say?

"But I chose my job. I could quit anytime." (And then what? Lose your house? Lose your car? Default on your loans? Watch your family starve?)

"But I chose where to live. I could move anywhere." (And do what? You need a job. You need income. You need to be near employment. Economic necessity limits your choices.)

"But I'm free. I can do whatever I want." (Can you? Can you really? Try opting out of car insurance. Try not paying property taxes. Try living off-grid without government permission. Try any true alternative, and you'll discover quickly how "free" you are.)

The slave defends his slavery because acknowledging the truth is too painful. Because seeing the chains means feeling their weight. Because recognizing enslavement means confronting the horrifying reality, that escape may cost everything.

This is hard. Sometimes it's the hardest thing a person will ever do. Those in bondage learn to love their chains, defend their captors, and ridicule anyone who suggests another way is possible.

'If only we had died by the Lord's hand in Egypt! There we sat around pots of meat and ate all the food we wanted.' (Exodus 16:3, NIV)

They wanted to return to slavery because freedom with God was uncomfortable. Freedom required daily trust, daily dependence on God, daily walking into the unknown. Slavery at least offered certainty.

"The Matrix"

There's a scene in the movie "The Matrix" where Morpheus says to Neo: "The Matrix is a system, Neo. That system is our enemy. But when you're inside, you look around, what do you see? Businessmen, teachers, lawyers, carpenters. The very minds of the people we are trying to save. But until we do, these people are still a part of that system, and that makes them our enemy. You have to understand, most of these people are not ready to be unplugged. And many of them are so inured, so hopelessly dependent on the system, that they will fight to protect it."

Now, the people are not our enemy, but this is reality described through story.

The people around you, John's coworkers, your family members, your friends, they are enslaved. And if you try to show them their chains, many will attack you for it. They will call you crazy, extreme, unrealistic, irresponsible.

Why? Because they are part of the system, and they will fight to protect it.

They will fight to protect the very system that enslaves them because acknowledging enslavement means acknowledging that they've wasted their entire lives serving a lie.

The Historical Pattern

Demanding a King:

God ruled Israel directly through judges. No human king. No centralized power taking from them. Relative freedom.

But the people looked at the nations around them and said, "We want a king like everyone else."
Samuel warned them exactly what would happen:

"He will take your sons and make them serve with his chariots and horses, and they will run in front of his chariots. Some he will assign to be commanders of thousands and commanders of fifties, and others to plow his ground and reap his harvest, and still others to make weapons of war and equipment for his chariots. He will take your daughters to be perfumers and cooks and bakers. He will take the best of your fields and vineyards and olive groves and give them to his attendants. He will take a tenth of your grain and of your vintage and give it to his officials and attendants. Your male and female servants and the best of your cattle and donkeys he will take for his own use. He will take a tenth of your flocks, and you yourselves will become his slaves. When that day comes, you will cry out for relief from the king you have chosen, but the Lord will not answer you in that day." (1 Samuel 8:11-18, NIV)

Read that again. Samuel laid out the entire system of greed: taking sons, taking daughters, taking fields, taking grain, taking flocks. The king would take from their lives exactly like Pharaoh did in Egypt.
And what was their response?

"But the people refused to listen to Samuel. 'No!' they said. 'We want a king over us. Then we will be like all the other nations.'" (1 Samuel 8:19-20, NIV)

They chose enslavement. God warned them. Samuel warned them. They didn't care.
Why? Because everyone else had a king. Because trusting human authority felt safer.

Because freedom required them to trust God, and that was too difficult.

So God gave them what they demanded. And they got exactly what Samuel warned: enslavement by their own choice.

The Cycle of Judges:
Before the kings, there was a pattern that repeated for generations. You can read it in the book of Judges:
-Israel has freedom
-They abandon God and serve other gods
-God allows a foreign nation to oppress them
-They cry out to God for deliverance
-God sends a judge (deliverer) who frees them
-They have freedom again
-They abandon God again
Over and over and over. The same cycle. Freedom, rebellion, enslavement, deliverance, freedom, rebellion, enslavement.

"In those days Israel had no king; everyone did as they saw fit." (Judges 21:25, NIV)

That sounds like freedom, doesn't it? No king. No tyrant. Everyone did as they saw fit.
But they couldn't handle it. Freedom required responsibility. Freedom required choosing God daily. Freedom required them to stand against darkness, resisting the temptation to serve the gods of the surrounding nations.
That was too hard. So they kept choosing slavery, not because someone forced them, but because freedom requires work, sacrifice, and moral conviction.

The Pattern Is Clear:
When freedom requires responsibility, slaves demand a tyrant to rule them. When freedom requires daily faithfulness, they repeatedly choose rebellion that leads back to enslavement.

This is Satan's pattern. He doesn't need to force you into chains. He just needs to make freedom uncomfortable enough that you put the chains back on yourself.

Just like John denied it. Just like you might deny it right now.

"I'm not enslaved."

" I have a good job."

" I chose this life."

"I'm free."

The Slavery You Can't See
Here's what makes modern slavery so effective: you can't see the chains. In Egypt, the chains were physical. Iron shackles. Armed guards. Physical barriers preventing escape.

In modern America, the chains are financial, legal, social, and psychological.

Financial chains: Debt that cannot be escaped. Interest that compounds faster than you can pay. Bills that never stop coming. A system designed to keep you perpetually behind.

Legal chains: Laws that make opting out illegal. Regulations that make alternatives impossible. Enforcement mechanisms that punish deviation. A cage made of statutes and codes.

Social chains: Expectations that must be met. Status that must be maintained. Judgments that must be avoided. A prison made of opinions and comparisons.

Demonic chains: Darkness planted in your mind from childhood. Thoughts you never chose but accepted as your own. Fear that paralyzes you. Lust that pulls you into the world. The bondage of contaminated thought itself.

These chains are invisible. You can't photograph them. You can't show them to anyone. You can't unlock them with a key.
But they're more effective than iron shackles ever were.
Because you can't fight what you don't acknowledge. You can't escape what you don't recognize as a cage. You can't break chains you don't believe exist.

The Connection Between the Two

Here's what most people miss: these two levels of slavery work together. The spiritual slavery (to sin) makes you vulnerable to the physical slavery (to systems).
Here's how:
Greed within you makes you susceptible to the system of debt. The bank doesn't force you to take a loan. They offer it. And the greed in you says, "Give it to me."
Fear within you makes you obey oppressive laws. The government doesn't have to physically force you to pay them. The demon of fear within you compels you to comply.
Pride within you makes you chase status and possessions. The corporations don't have to force you to buy. Pride wants to have better things than others.
Lust within you makes you pursue things designed to stimulate pleasure. The demons know exactly which buttons to push.

The external systems of slavery only work because of the internal contamination of sin.

If you weren't greedy, debt wouldn't tempt you. If you weren't fearful, hate wouldn't control you. If you weren't proud, possessions wouldn't enslave you. If you weren't lustful, desire wouldn't manipulate you.

This is why Jesus said the truth will set you free. The truth about the external systems that enslave you. The truth about the internal contamination that blinds you. Both must be seen.

You are enslaved from within before you are enslaved from without.

And this is why mere political revolution never works. This is why overthrowing governments or corporations or banks won't free you.

Because as long as the hearts of people are contaminated by sin, they will just rebuild the same systems of slavery under new names.

The French Revolution overthrew a monarchy and created a dictatorship. The Russian Revolution overthrew a czar and created a totalitarian state. The American Revolution overthrew British rule and created a system that still enslaves through taxation.

Every revolution that doesn't address the spiritual contamination just replaces one puppet of darkness with another.

The Only Path to Freedom

So what's the answer? How do you break free from this slavery?

There's only one way: Surrender to the Father.

Not "Christianity" as a religion. Not "church" as an institution. Not "belief" as mental acceptance.

But the Father, God Himself, who alone has the authority and power to break every chain that binds you.

Jesus declared this truth plainly: *"So if the Son sets you free, you will be free indeed."* (John 8:36, NIV)

Notice the word "indeed." Not partially free. Not kind of free. Not free in theory. Free INDEED. Truly free. Actually free. Completely free.

But understand what Jesus is saying: the Son sets you free. Not your effort. Not your willpower. Not your good intentions. The Son is the one with the power to break the chains. And He does this on behalf of the Father, to bring you into the Father's family.

This is why Jesus said, *"No one comes to the Father except through me."* (John 14:6, NIV) The path to the Father's freedom runs through the Son's sacrifice.

But this freedom comes at a cost that few are willing to pay. What that cost looks like, how it's paid, and why it's worth everything, we'll explore ahead.

For now, know this: the Father doesn't free you so you can remain the same person. He frees you to transform you.

John's Choice, Your Choice

Let's go back to John for a moment.

John is enslaved. Financially, legally, socially, psychologically, spiritually. He needs to work 27 days out of every 21 to survive. He goes deeper into debt every month. He has no margin, no freedom, no peace.

But John also has a choice.

He can continue as he is, believing the lie that he's free, defending the system that enslaves him, teaching his children to pursue the same slavery.

Or he can see the truth, acknowledge his chains, and begin the arduous process of breaking free.

What would breaking free look like for John?

It would mean confronting the spiritual contamination within himself first. Acknowledging that he's not just prey of systems, but a willing participant in sin. Repenting. Confessing with his mouth and turning to the Father.

"If we confess our sins, he is faithful and just and will forgive us our sins and purify us from all unrighteousness." (1 John 1:9, NIV)

It would mean making different choices. Choices that the world would call foolish. Choices that might cost him everything the world values. Maybe it means walking away from the job that demands he compromise his integrity. Maybe it means selling the house and the cars and getting out of debt, even if it means "downgrading." Maybe it means trusting God for provision instead of trusting man. Maybe it means living radically differently than everyone around him.

The specifics would be between John and God. But the principle is universal: freedom requires sacrifice. True freedom requires dying to the world.

And this is your choice too.

You can continue reading this book as an interesting intellectual exercise, then close it and go back to your enslaved life, nothing changed.

Or you can let the truth of what you're reading penetrate your heart, break you, and remake you into someone who refuses to serve the tyrant any longer.

The choice is yours.

But know this: you cannot serve two masters.

"No one can serve two masters. Either you will hate the one and love the other, or you will be devoted to the one and despise the other. You cannot serve both God and money." (Matthew 6:24, NIV)

THE TYRANT

You cannot serve God and the system. You cannot serve light and darkness. You cannot be free and enslaved.
You must choose.

The Tragedy of Wasted Lives
I want to end this chapter with the most sobering reality of all.
Most people will read this, feel uncomfortable for a moment, and then return to their slavery unchanged.
Most people, when faced with the truth of their enslavement, will choose to remain enslaved rather than sacrifice the temporary discomfort for permanent (eternal) freedom.
Most people will spend their entire lives serving the tyrant, enriching greed, feeding hate, obeying fear, and they will die having had every opportunity to choose life.

And on the day of judgment, when they stand before God and say *"Lord, Lord,"* He may say, *"I never knew you. Away from me, you evildoers!"*
Not because they didn't believe in God. Not because they didn't go to church. Not because they didn't say the right prayers.

But because they spent their lives serving the wrong master.

They served each other. They served the world. They served the tyrant. They served sin.
And they called it "responsibility." They called it "being realistic." They called it "providing for my family." They called it "being a good citizen."

But God calls it what it is: Slavery.
And slaves do not inherit the kingdom.

"Now a slave has no permanent place in the family, but a son belongs to it forever." (John 8:35, NIV)

If you live as a slave, you die as a slave. And slaves don't inherit.
Only sons and daughters inherit. Only those who have been set free by the Son inherit. Only those who have died to this world and been born again into God's kingdom inherit.

This is the truth about slavery.
This is the reality you must face.
This is the choice you must make.
Will you remain a slave? Or will you be set free?

The answer to that question will determine not just the quality of your life here, but the destination of your spirit for eternity.

Choose wisely.

But I know what you're probably thinking. I know the question rising in your heart right now:
If this is true, if God sees this enslavement, if He loves His people... why doesn't He end it? Why does He allow this tyranny to continue?

This is the right question. And the answer in the next part will change everything you understand about suffering, pressure, and what God is actually doing in your life right now.

PART SIX: THE MODEL OF TYRANNY

The Historical Pattern: God's People Under Tyranny

You've seen it now. You've seen your enslavement, your chains, the illusion of choice. Now you're ready for the question everyone asks: Why does God allow this?

This is not new. The enslavement you experience, the tyranny that surrounds you, the systems that take from your life, none of this is unique to your generation.

God's people have always lived under tyranny. Consistently. This is the pattern throughout all of Scripture, throughout all of human history. And in every instance, God doesn't immediately remove the tyrant. Instead, He refines His people through the pressure of tyranny.

Egypt: The Slavery of Bricks

Egyptians enslaved the Israelites for 400 years. Families who never knew freedom, who were born into bondage, who died in bondage, who watched their children born into the same bondage.

Pharaoh forced them to make bricks. To build cities. To labor until exhaustion. The Bible records the brutal quotas:

"That same day Pharaoh gave this order to the slave drivers and overseers in charge of the people: 'You are no longer to supply the people with straw for making bricks; let them go and gather their own straw. But require them to make the same number of bricks as before; don't reduce the quota.'" (Exodus 5:6-8, NIV)

Work harder. Produce more. With fewer resources. Sound familiar? This is John's life. This is your life. The same pattern, thousands of years later.

And where was God during those 400 years? Was He absent? Had He forgotten His people?

No, He was refining them. Forging their identity as His people. When God finally sent Moses to deliver them, they knew beyond doubt that their freedom came from God alone, not from their own strength or wisdom.

The slavery in Egypt created a dependence on God that prosperity never could have produced. Though that generation died in the wilderness, their children entered the promised land knowing that freedom came from God alone, not from their own strength.

Babylon: The Exile That Purified Worship

Centuries later, Israel finally had its own nation, its own land, its own temple, and they fell into sin. They worshiped idols instead of God. They oppressed the poor while maintaining the religious rituals of other nations. They contaminated the pure worship God had given them with the idolatry of other nations.

So God allowed Babylon to conquer them. Nebuchadnezzar destroyed Jerusalem, burned the temple, and carried the people into exile. For 70 years, they lived in a foreign land, under a foreign king, serving a foreign empire.

They threw Daniel into a den of lions because he prayed to God. They threw Shadrach, Meshach, and Abednego into a furnace heated seven times hotter than normal because they refused to bow to an idol. It was so hot that it killed the men who threw them into the furnace.

King Nebuchadnezzar himself watched what happened next:

"Look! I see four men walking around in the fire, unbound and unharmed, and the fourth looks like a son of the gods." (Daniel 3:25, NIV)

When they emerged from the furnace:
"The fire had not harmed their bodies, nor was a hair of their heads singed; their robes were not scorched, and there was no smell of fire on them." (Daniel 3:27, NIV)

The people of God lived under constant threat, constant oppression, and constant tyranny.
And where was God?
Right there in the furnace with Shadrach, Meshach, and Abednego.
Right there in the lions' den with Daniel. Right there in Babylon with His people.

"So the king gave the order, and they brought Daniel and threw him into the lions' den. The king said to Daniel, 'May your God, whom you serve continually, rescue you!' ... When Daniel was lifted from the den, no wound was found on him, because he had trusted in his God." (Daniel 6:16, 23, NIV)

The exile refined Israel's trust in God. The pressure of Babylon accomplished what prosperity never could; it broke their attraction to foreign gods and drove them back to dependence on the God who delivered them.

Only when you lose everything do you discover what you truly needed.

Rome: The Occupation That Prepared for a New Message

Fast forward to the time of Jesus. Israel was under Roman occupation. They were enslaved again, this time by Rome. Caesar demanded taxes.

Roman soldiers patrolled their streets. Their own religious leaders collaborated with the occupiers to maintain power.

The people were waiting for a Messiah to free them. To overthrow Rome. To establish an earthly kingdom where Israel would rule.

Jesus came. But He didn't overthrow Rome. He didn't establish an earthly kingdom. Instead, He offered something far more radical: **freedom.**

"Jesus replied, 'Very truly I tell you, everyone who sins is a slave to sin. Now a slave has no permanent place in the family, but a son belongs to it forever. So if the Son sets you free, you will be free indeed.'" (John 8:34-36, NIV)

The people couldn't understand. They wanted political freedom. Jesus offered eternal freedom. They wanted Rome removed. Jesus offered sin removed.

Why? Because God was using Rome's tyranny to prepare His people for a spiritual kingdom. The pressure of the occupation made them cry out for a deliverer. And the Deliverer came, but not the one they expected. He came to deliver them from something far worse than Rome: from sin itself, from death itself, from Satan himself.

Rome crucified Jesus. And in that act of ultimate tyranny, God accomplished ultimate redemption. The tyrant's greatest weapon, death, became the message of eternal life.

The Modern System

Now look at your time. You live under a different kind of tyranny. The chains of debt, not Pharaoh's whips. Not Nebuchadnezzar's decree, but the government's regulations. Not Caesar's taxation, but a system that extracts 62% of your life before you can even think about survival.

This is the same pattern. Different forms, same function. Tyranny refining God's people.

THE TYRANT

Just as Egypt couldn't enslave Israel's spirit, just as Babylon couldn't destroy their identity, just as Rome couldn't prevent Jesus from coming, the modern system cannot enslave your spirit unless you let it.

The tyrant can take your money. He can regulate your actions. He can fill your life with stress and debt and fear. But he cannot contaminate your spirit unless you allow it.

The Pattern Is Clear

Enslavement is not the exception; it's the rule. God's people have always lived under tyranny. And in every case, God used that tyranny to:

-Refine their faith

-Purify their worship

-Prepare them for His kingdom

-Reveal who truly chooses Him

You are living in the same pattern. The financial slavery you experience, the regulatory cage you're trapped in, the greed that takes from your life, this is your Egypt, your Babylon, your Rome.

And God is using it to refine you. To purify you. To prepare you. To filter you.

The question is not "Why doesn't God remove the tyrant?"

The question is: "What is God producing in me through this pressure? Will I let Him refine me, or will I waste the fire by choosing the world instead of Him?"

Why God Allows This

Because the greatest prize ever offered requires the greatest commitment.

Eternal life. A kingdom without darkness. Perfect love without contamination. An existence beyond what your mind can comprehend. This is not given to the casual. This is not handed to the lazy. This is not awarded to those who coast across the finish line.

"The kingdom of heaven has been forcefully advancing, and forceful men lay hold of it." (Matthew 11:12, NIV)

God gives you a choice. Life or death. Good or evil. Light or darkness. You face both every single day, every single moment.

"This day I call the heavens and the earth as witnesses against you that I have set before you life and death, blessings and curses. Now choose life, so that you and your children may live." (Deuteronomy 30:19, NIV)

The choice is yours. Not God's. Not Satan's. Yours.
You must choose life with everything within you. You must fight for it. You must pursue it relentlessly. You must stand against the darkness that surrounds you and say, "No, I choose God. I choose life."

This is not cruelty from God. This is love.

Because a kingdom as holy, as pure, as perfect as the one He offers cannot be polluted with those who took instead of gave. It cannot be contaminated by those who chose darkness. It cannot include those who gave their lives to the tyrant. The very spirit of the person would contaminate heaven, and heaven itself would fall.

This isn't a punishment of God. It is a consequence of sin.

Remember: diamonds are formed under extreme pressure. Your spirit is being refined under the extreme pressure of this life. The darkness that surrounds you, the enslavement that binds you, the greed that takes from you: these are the weights that forge something in you that could not exist without them.

"Consider it pure joy, my brothers and sisters, whenever you face trials of many kinds, because you know that the testing of your faith produces perseverance. Let perseverance finish its work so that you may be mature and complete, not lacking anything." (James 1:2-4, NIV)

God allows this because He is creating something in you. Something beautiful. Something eternal. Something that can only be formed through struggle, through choice, through standing against darkness when every fiber of your being wants to give in.

You are being refined. And God walks with you through every moment of that refining fire.

The Question Everyone Asks
But this raises the question that every person asks when they see the depth of enslavement, the completeness of tyranny, the suffering of the innocent:
If God is all-powerful, if God is loving, if God is just, why doesn't He just end this? Why doesn't He destroy Satan right now? Why doesn't He remove the tyrant, break the chains, free His people immediately?

This is not a new question. This is the question Job asked when he lost everything. This is the question the psalmist asked: *'How long, Lord? Will you forget me forever?'* (Psalm 13:1, NIV) This is the question Jesus' disciples asked: *'Lord, are you at this time going to restore the kingdom to Israel?'* (Acts 1:6, NIV)
The answer is not simple. But it is profound. And understanding it will change how you see every moment of suffering, every pressure, every trial.

Answer 1: Love Requires Giving Choice

God could force you to choose Him. He could override your will, eliminate your ability to choose darkness, make you a puppet who only does good.

But that wouldn't be love. That would just be another tyrant.

Love requires the freedom to choose. If you cannot choose to reject God, then your choice to accept God is meaningless. If you cannot choose darkness, then choosing light has no value.

"This day I call the heavens and the earth as witnesses against you that I have set before you life and death, blessings and curses. Now choose life, so that you and your children may live." (Deuteronomy 30:19, NIV)

God set before you both options. Not just life, but also death. Not just blessings, but also curses. Why? Because the choice must be real.
If God removed Satan right now, if He eliminated all darkness, all evil, all temptation, you would have no choice. You would default to good not because you chose it, but because it's the only option available.
And God doesn't want slaves. He wants sons and daughters who choose Him freely, who love Him voluntarily, who serve Him because they want to, not because they have to.

This is why the tyrant still exists. Not because God is weak, but because God is loving. He's giving you the freedom to choose.

Answer 2: Pressure Refines the Spirit

Here's what most people don't understand: you don't know who you really are until you're under pressure.

THE TYRANT

When life is easy, when money flows, when health is good, when circumstances are favorable, everyone looks righteous. Everyone can be generous when they have excess. Everyone can be patient when nothing tests them. Everyone can claim faith when there's nothing to test that faith against.

But pressure reveals the truth. Pressure shows what's really inside.

"In this you greatly rejoice, though now for a little while you may have had to suffer grief in all kinds of trials. These have come so that the proven genuineness of your faith—of greater worth than gold, which perishes even though refined by fire—may result in praise, glory and honor when Jesus Christ is revealed." (1 Peter 1:6-7, NIV)

Gold is refined by fire. The heat doesn't create the impurities; it reveals them. The impurities were always there, hidden in the ore. The fire just reveals them, allowing for their removal.

The pressure of this world, the tyranny you experience, the enslavement you live under, this is the fire that reveals what's really in you.

When the pressure comes, do you choose greed or generosity? When the fear rises, do you trust God or trust the world? When you're surrounded by hate, do you respond with love or retaliate? When darkness offers you comfort, do you choose light even when it costs you everything?

These questions cannot be answered in theory. Answering them is possible only under pressure.

God is not torturing you. He's revealing you. He's showing you whether your faith is real or just words. Whether your love for Him is genuine or just convenient. Whether you truly choose Him in all things or only choose Him when it's convenient.

The tyrant's pressure is the furnace that refines gold. God, the Master Refiner, knows exactly how much heat is needed, and for how long, to produce something pure.

Answer 3: The Separation of Wheat and Chaff

Jesus told a parable about wheat and weeds growing together:

"The kingdom of heaven is like a man who sowed good seed in his field. But while everyone was sleeping, his enemy came and sowed weeds among the wheat, and went away. When the wheat sprouted and formed heads, then the weeds also appeared. The owner's servants came to him and said, 'Sir, didn't you sow good seed in your field? Where then did the weeds come from?' 'An enemy did this,' he replied. The servants asked him, 'Do you want us to go and pull them up?' 'No,' he answered, 'because while you are pulling the weeds, you may uproot the wheat with them. Let both grow together until the harvest. At that time I will tell the harvesters: First collect the weeds and tie them in bundles to be burned; then gather the wheat and bring it into my barn.'" (Matthew 13:24-30, NIV)

The weeds are those who belong to the tyrant. The wheat are those who belong to God. And right now, they're growing together in the same field.

The servants want to pull up the weeds immediately. That seems right. That seems just. Why let evil grow alongside good?

But God says no, not yet. Let them both grow. Why? 'Because while you are pulling the weeds, you may uproot the wheat with them.'

Here's what this means: if God destroyed evil right now, if He removed all darkness, all evil, all contamination, some of His own children would be destroyed in the process. Because they're contaminated. Because they're still serving greed, still enslaved to fear, still compromised by pride. Right now, weeds contaminate them, but they still have a chance to become wheat. God will give them every opportunity.

God is waiting. Not because He's slow. Not because He's weak. But because He's patient. He's giving every possible person every possible chance to choose Him before the harvest comes.

"The Lord is not slow in keeping his promise, as some understand slowness. Instead he is patient with you, not wanting anyone to perish, but everyone to come to repentance." (2 Peter 3:9, NIV)

Every day the tyrant remains is another day for someone to wake up. Another day for someone to see their chains. Another day for someone to choose life instead of death.

God is not delaying Justice. He's extending mercy.

Answer 4: Satan's Lease Has an Expiration Date
Here's what you must understand: this is temporary.
Satan's influence in this world is real, but it's limited. God has allowed him to rule for a season, but that season has an end date.
The Bible is clear about this:

"And the devil, who deceived them, was thrown into the lake of burning sulfur, where the beast and the false prophet had been thrown. They will be tormented day and night for ever and ever." (Revelation 20:10, NIV)

Satan will be destroyed. The tyrant will fall. The systems of greed and hate will burn. Every chain will be broken. Every slave will be freed.
But not yet.
Why not now? Because God is still writing the story. He's still refining His people. He's still separating wheat from chaff. He's still extending mercy to those who haven't chosen yet.

When the time is right, when every person who will choose God has chosen Him, when the wheat is fully mature, when the harvest is ready, God will act. And it will be swift. And it will be final. And it will be complete.

"For the Lord himself will come down from heaven, with a loud command, with the voice of the archangel and with the trumpet call of God, and the dead in Christ will rise first. After that, we who are still alive and are left will be caught up together with them in the clouds to meet the Lord in the air. And so we will be with the Lord forever." (1 Thessalonians 4:16-17, NIV)

The tyrant's days are numbered. Your enslavement has an expiration date. The suffering is temporary. The kingdom is eternal.
This is why God allows it: because He's using this temporary pressure to create eternal glory in you.

So the question is not 'Why doesn't God end this now?
The question is: "What is God creating in me through this pressure that could not be created any other way?"'

The Model of Tyranny: How It Spreads
You understand WHY God allows tyranny. Now you need to see HOW it operates. Once you see the pattern, you'll recognize it everywhere: in your workplace, your government, your own actions. You'll see how contamination spreads, how the enslaved become enslavers, how the system perpetuates itself across generations.

Step 1: Contaminate the thinking

Satan simply needs to contaminate your thinking. Make you believe that greed is normal. That fear is prudence. That greed is survival. That hate is justified.

When your thinking is contaminated, you enslave yourself. You become the tyrant's tool without even knowing it.

Step 2: The enslaved become the enslavers

John is enslaved by the bank, by the dealership, by the insurance company, by the government. But what does John do?

He goes to work and manages people below him. He demands productivity. He enforces rules. He becomes, in his own small way, a tyrant to those beneath him in the chain.

The landlord was once a renter. The boss was once an employee. The one taking is also the one being taken from. Everyone in the system is both prey and predator.

This is how tyranny spreads. Not through force alone, but through contamination. The enslaved learn the model and apply it to those they can control.

Step 3: Call it freedom

The greatest deception is making you believe you chose this. That you're free. That this is normal, the way things should be.

"I chose this job."

"I chose this house."

"I chose this life."

You call it freedom while you wear chains. You defend the system that enslaves you. You teach your children to pursue the same enslavement and call it success.

This is the model. This is how it spreads. Generation after generation, person after person, contaminated thinking created contaminated systems for contaminated people.

Step 4: Use fear to maintain control

The tyrant does not rule by love. The tyrant rules by fear.

Fear of losing your job. Fear of losing your house. Fear of going to jail. Fear of fines, penalties, consequences. Fear of not having enough. Fear of being left behind. Fear of not being good enough.

Fear keeps you working. Fear keeps you paying. Fear keeps you obeying. And fear is contagious. Like a disease, it spreads. The fearful create more fear in those around them.

The Pattern Across All Levels

Look at the government. Federal, state, county, city. All operate on the same model: create rules, enforce with fear, extract payment, call it protection.

Look at corporations. CEO, management, supervisors, workers. All operate on the same model: demand productivity, threaten consequences, take the surplus, call it employment.

Look at banks. Lend money that doesn't exist, charge interest, threaten foreclosure (take it from you), call it service.

Look at every level of this system and you see the same pattern: contaminated thinking, enslavement of those below, fear as control, greed as motive.

This is not random. This is not accidental. This is coordinated, and it's worldwide.

Not by human collusion. It would be impossible for any human to coordinate such enslavement worldwide. This is spiritual contamination. The same dark force influences every level, every person, every institution. All operating under the same model. All serving the same master, whether or not they know it.

But You Are Not Without Hope

This is the world you live in. This is the system you were born into. This is the tyranny that surrounds you.

But you are not powerless. You are not without a choice. You are not without God.

Every moment you stand against the darkness, you refine your spirit. Every time you choose to give instead of take, to love instead of hate, to serve instead of enslave, you are fighting for eternal life.

God walks with you in this fight. He sees every choice. He knows every struggle. He is refining you for something greater than this temporary world.

So now you understand: "Why does God allow this?" is the wrong question.

The real question is: "What will you do with the choice He's given you?"

Will you give in to the contamination? Will you become another link in the chain of tyranny? Will you enslave others because you are enslaved?

Or will you stand? Will you fight? Will you choose life, even when surrounded by death?

This is the model of tyranny. And this is the choice before you.

Will you see it? Or will you remain blind?

Will you recognize the contamination in your own thinking, in your own actions, in your own participation in this system? Or will you continue to believe you're innocent, that you're just surviving, that you have no choice?

You do have a choice. You've always had a choice.

But first, you must accept the depth of your enslavement. You must see that the slavery you live under is not just economic.
It's not just political. It's not just social:
It's spiritual.

PART SEVEN: THE ONLY HOPE

What You Must Do

So what now? Now that you see the tyrant. Now that you see your chains. Now that you understand that enslavement is not just physical but spiritual. What do you do?

You cannot overthrow this tyrant with violence. You cannot vote him out. You cannot protest him away. You cannot reform the system he's built because it is contaminated at its foundation.

There is only one path to freedom: Die to this world.

You already know what this means. We've covered the theology. Now it's time for the practice.

This will cost you everything. Your comfort. Your security. Your plans. Your future as you imagined it.

But here's what the tyrant doesn't want you to know: What you lose here, you gain eternally.

The Theft of a Gift

Here's something you may not have known. God wants to provide for us. God wants to give to us. But when Satan entered the world, his mere presence meant enslavement for all of God's children. He would not allow God to provide for His children. Satan's goal was to enslave the creation and make them fight over what God had already given for free. Make them dedicate their entire lives to obtaining what God had given freely.

Satan is a thief, and he contaminated the creation and enslaved all of God's children.

The fantastic news is God wants to give to His children.

This is the deception of darkness: that God wields the mighty hammer of oppression. All of these consequences came from Satan entering the creation. This was the consequence of darkness alone, not God. And this is what Satan does to the creation, he contaminates the mind, corrupts the thoughts, twists the beliefs. You can read the Bible itself and not see the truth within it because of the darkness within your own mind, thoughts contaminated by hate, pride, and all the other demons that followed him into the creation.

Satan's first and greatest contamination was convincing you of one simple lie.

I Need.

This is the lie. This is the deception.

"I need food. I need clothing. I need a house. I need a car. I need a job." God owns everything. It is all His. Every tree, every grain of wheat, every resource on this planet belongs to Him. When you say, "I need," greed is whispering in your ear, telling you to *take* from God what He wants to *give* to you.

That's right. God wants to give to you. God wants to provide.

You have lived your whole life believing there are wants and needs. You were taught to fight, claw, and provide for your needs. These are non-negotiable, they told you. Survival justifies anything.

But this is a lie.

Greed takes and takes and takes. You have taken from people your whole life to support the lie of "I need," and you called it life. You manipulated. You hoarded. You stepped on others. You exploited. You charged interest. You demanded payment. You competed against brothers and sisters all because of "I need."

This is how darkness has destroyed the creation, by convincing God's children to take from one another instead of receiving from their Father.

This is why Jesus said: *"Give, and it will be given to you. A good measure, pressed down, shaken together and running over, will be poured into your lap. For with the measure you use, it will be measured to you."* (Luke 6:38)

He wasn't teaching generosity as a nice virtue. He was exposing the fundamental lie of greed, the deception that says you must take to survive. Jesus commanded giving because it breaks the influence of "I need."

When you give, you declare God provides.
When you take, you declare no need for God.

The entire economic system is built on the lie of need. Satan convinced humanity that resources are scarce, that you must compete for survival, that taking from others is justified because "I need." And once that lie took root, greed built an empire. Banks, interest, wages, rent, taxes, all of it flows from the original deception: "You are on your own. God will not provide. You must take."

But Jesus said: *"Look at the birds of the air; they do not sow or reap or store away in barns, and yet your heavenly Father feeds them. Are you not much more valuable than they?"* (Matthew 6:26)

The kingdom of God operates on giving. The kingdom of darkness operates on taking. Every time you say, "I need," you serve the latter. And what you pursue reveals which kingdom you serve:

"Do not store up for yourselves treasures on earth, where moths and vermin destroy... But store up for yourselves treasures in heaven... For where your treasure is, there your heart will be also." (Matthew 6:19-21, NIV)

Everything the tyrant offers you is temporary. Everything God offers you is eternal.
The house? Temporary. The car? Temporary. The job? Temporary. The money? Temporary. The pleasure? Temporary. Your very life in this flesh? Temporary.

"What good is it for someone to gain the whole world, yet forfeit their soul?" (Mark 8:36, NIV)

The tyrant wants you to gain the world. He wants you enslaved to it. He wants you working for it, fighting for it, dying for it. Because as long as you're focused on gaining the world, you cannot gain what matters.

What Blocks Provision
This is the hard part though. You will always be enslaved within the flesh unless you walk with God in obedience 100%. You cannot have self-reliance through pride, greed, fear, or selfishness, and expect God to provide for you.

-Greed says, "Take."
-Pride says, "I can do this."

THE TYRANT

-Fear says, "You better work or you're going to starve."
-Selfishness whispers, "Keep it all to yourself."
-Hate says, "I don't care about anyone else."

God cannot bless through all of this darkness. He cannot give through all of this. If He gave, He would be giving directly to darkness.
So how do you release this? How do you purge yourself of all the contamination in the flesh?
What did Jesus say?

"If you want to be perfect, go, sell your possessions and give to the poor, and you will have treasure in heaven. Then come, follow me." (Matthew 19:21, NIV)

Losing Everything to Gain Everything
You must lose everything. If pride has nothing to hold on to, it won't stay. If the fear of losing a job keeps fear within you, you have to walk away from the job. If greed says take more and you take nothing, what purpose does greed now have? If hate says, "I'm going to destroy your life," and you strip everything that you ever had from your life, hate has no more power.
Only through losing everything in the flesh can you truly be freed from enslavement.
How many are really able to do all of this? How many that walk now on this earth are willing and have a heart to give it all to God? This is hard right! Only in giving it all to Him and losing it all can you be freed from the darkness within you.

"Whoever wants to be my disciple must deny themselves and take up their cross and follow me. For whoever wants to save their life will lose it, but whoever loses their life for me will find it." (Matthew 16:24-25, NIV)

This is the truth that the churches won't preach. This is the cost that no one wants to pay. This is the freedom that looks like death to the enslaved.

But it is the only freedom that exists.

If you lose the world, if you walk away from the enslavement, if you refuse to bow to the systems of greed and hate, if you give away what the tyrant tells you to keep, you gain everything.

This is the promise. This is the hope. This is the only path to freedom.

The Last Choice

You stand at a crossroads now. You've seen the tyrant. You've seen your chains. You can't erase what was revealed.

You have two choices:

Choice One: Close this book. Go back to your life. Wake up tomorrow, check your phone, drink your coffee, go to work, pay your bills, and pretend you are free. The tyrant will welcome you back. The chains will feel comfortable again. You will forget what you read here, or you will dismiss it as extreme, as unrealistic, as impossible to live.

And you will remain enslaved until the day you die. The wide path you chose will contaminate your spirit. And when you stand before God, you will say, "Lord, Lord, I believed in you." And He will say, "I never knew you."

Choice Two: Act. Today. Now. Each person's path is guided by God. But we know from Scripture you must begin dying to this world. Give away what you're holding onto. Walk away from what enslaves you. Stop participating in the tyrant's system. Choose love when hate whispers. Choose giving when greed screams. Choose trust when fear paralyzes.

This choice will cost you everything in this life. Your family may not understand. Your friends may abandon you. The world will call you foolish. The tyrant will attack you with everything he has.

But you will be free. Truly free. Free in your spirit. Free from darkness's grasp. Free for eternity.

The tyrant's power is an illusion. His influence is temporary. His chains only bind those who choose them.

But God's kingdom is eternal. His freedom is real. His promise is sure. Choose wisely. Choose today. Choose life.

Tomorrow is not promised.
And the tyrant?
He's counting on you waiting until tomorrow.
Because tomorrow never comes.

What Dying to the World Looks Like

The cage has been shown through Scripture. The chains have been documented in God's Word. The tyrant has been named from Genesis to Revelation. And Scripture is clear: you must die to this world to be free.

But what does that actually mean? What does it look like in real life, in practical terms, in daily choices?

Let me show you what dying to the world looks like through the only examples that matter: real people from Scripture who actually did it. Not hypothetical scenarios. Not made-up stories. The choices of real people were recorded so we could learn from them.

Moses: Walking Away from Royalty

Moses was raised as the son of Pharaoh's daughter. He had everything: wealth, power, education, privilege, security. He was in a long line to potentially rule Egypt, the most powerful empire on earth at that time.

Moses could have lived in luxury for his entire life. He could have had servants, palaces, anything he wanted. He was set for life by worldly standards.

But Hebrews 11:24-26 tells us what Moses chose:

"By faith Moses, when he had grown up, refused to be known as the son of Pharaoh's daughter. He chose to be mistreated along with the people of God rather than to enjoy the fleeting pleasures of sin. He regarded disgrace for the sake of Christ as of greater value than the treasures of Egypt, because he was looking ahead to his reward."

Read that again. Moses REFUSED the position. He CHOSE mistreatment. He regarded DISGRACE as more valuable than TREASURES.

This is what dying to the world looks like.

Moses walked away from a palace to live in the desert. He walked away from power to become a shepherd. He walked away from luxury to lead God's people through 40 years in the wilderness.

The world would say Moses was insane. The world would say he threw his life away. The world would say he made the worst decision possible.

But God says Moses was one of the most faithful men who ever lived.

What did Moses gain? Freedom from Egyptian contamination. The privilege and honor of speaking face-to-face with God. A purpose that changed human history. Eternal reward that no treasure of Egypt could match.

Moses looked ahead to his reward. He saw past the temporary to the eternal.

THE TYRANT

The Rich Young Ruler: The Man Who Couldn't Let Go
Now look at the opposite. Look at what happens when you choose the world over the kingdom.
In Matthew 19:16-22, a rich young man came to Jesus and asked what he must do to get eternal life. Jesus told him to keep the commandments. The young man said he'd kept them all and asked what he still lacked.

"Jesus answered, 'If you want to be perfect, go, sell your possessions and give to the poor, and you will have treasure in heaven. Then come, follow me.' When the young man heard this, he went away sad, because he had great wealth."

This man had everything by worldly standards: youth, wealth, religious devotion, moral behavior. He kept all the commandments. He was a "good person."

But he had one problem: he loved his wealth more than he loved God.

Jesus didn't tell him to sell his possessions because having money is inherently evil. Jesus told him to sell his possessions because Jesus could see what the man couldn't: his wealth OWNED him. The man didn't own his wealth; he was enslaved by it.
The man was proud of his obedience to the commandments. Proud of his moral record. Proud of being righteous. But his pride blinded him to who he was truly serving.

When forced to choose between his money and eternal life, he chose his money.

He went away sad.

Think about that. He had a face-to-face invitation from Jesus Christ himself, standing right in front of him, offering him eternal life, asking him to follow, and he said no because he couldn't let go of his stuff.

This is the tragedy of choosing the world. You gain everything the world offers, and you lose your life.

Jesus said immediately after this: *"Truly I tell you, it is hard for someone who is rich to enter the kingdom of heaven. Again I tell you, it is easier for a camel to go through the eye of a needle than for someone who is rich to enter the kingdom of God."* (Matthew 19:23-24)

Why? Because wealth is hoarding God's resources. Wealth is faith in self, not God. Wealth makes you think you don't need God. Wealth becomes your master without you even realizing it.

The rich young ruler had everything, and he had nothing. He clung to what he could see and forfeited what he could not. Moses lost everything and gained God. The rich young ruler kept everything and lost God. You will never know the young ruler's name. He chose death, and the living don't remember the dead.

Zacchaeus: The Tax Collector

Zacchaeus was the opposite of the rich young ruler. Zacchaeus was a chief tax collector, meaning he was rich from extorting his own people. People hated him. He was a collaborator with Rome. He was the personification of greed.

But when Jesus called him down from the tree and went to his house, something broke inside Zacchaeus.

"Zacchaeus stood up and said to the Lord, 'Look, Lord! Here and now I give half of my possessions to the poor, and if I have cheated anybody out of anything, I will pay back four times the amount.'" (Luke 19:8)

Zacchaeus didn't just give a little. He gave HALF of everything he owned to the poor. And then he paid back FOUR TIMES what he had stolen.

Do the math. If Zacchaeus had cheated people out of 25% of his wealth over the years (a conservative estimate for a corrupt tax collector), paying it back four times would cost him 100% of that wealth. Plus, he gave away half of what remained.

Zacchaeus committed to giving away 75-90% of everything he owned that day.

Why? Because he encountered Jesus. And when you truly encounter Jesus, you cannot hold on to the world.

"Today salvation has come to this house." (Luke 19:9)

Salvation came when Zacchaeus opened his hands. Freedom came when he made restitution. Life came when he gave back what he'd stolen, even though it cost him everything he'd accumulated. This is what repentance looks like in action, not words, not saying God exists, not religious ritual, but releasing your grip on the world.

The Early Church: Holding Nothing as Their Own
Acts 2:44-45 describes the early church:

"All the believers were together and had everything in common. They sold property and possessions to give to anyone who had need."

And Acts 4:32-35:
"All the believers were one in heart and mind. No one claimed that any of their possessions was their own, but they shared everything they had... There were no needy persons among them. For from time to time those who

owned land or houses sold them, brought the money from the sales and put it at the apostles' feet, and it was distributed to anyone who had need."

Read that carefully. *"No one claimed that any of their possessions was their own."*
This wasn't communism enforced by the government. This was love overflowing from hearts that had been transformed by the love of God. They SOLD their property. They GAVE to anyone in need. They shared EVERYTHING.

And what was the result? *"There were no needy persons among them."*

This is the heart of God in action. This is what the church looks like when it actually follows the Father instead of following the world. Why don't we see this today?

Because the modern church has been contaminated by the world.

Because we love our houses and our cars and our comfort more than we love God. Because we've been taught the lie of prosperity instead of the truth of sacrifice.
The early church had nothing and experienced everything. We have everything and experience nothing. They gave all and saw God move in power. We give leftovers and wonder why we're spiritually dead.

Paul: Losing Everything to Gain Christ
The Apostle Paul had credentials. He was a Pharisee, a scholar, a Roman citizen, educated under Gamaliel, blameless under the law. He had status, respect, power, and a future in the religious establishment.
But in Philippians 3:7-8, Paul says:

"Whatever were gains to me I now consider loss for the sake of Christ. What is more, I consider everything a loss because of the surpassing worth of knowing Christ Jesus my Lord, for whose sake I have lost all things. I consider them garbage, that I may gain Christ."

Paul lost everything. His status, his career, his reputation, his security. He was beaten, imprisoned, shipwrecked, stoned, mocked, rejected. In 2 Corinthians 11:23-27, Paul lists what dying to the world cost him:

"I have worked much harder, been in prison more frequently, been flogged more severely, and been exposed to death again and again. Five times I received from the Jews the forty lashes minus one. Three times I was beaten with rods, once I was pelted with stones, three times I was shipwrecked, I spent a night and a day in the open sea... I have known hunger and thirst and have often gone without food; I have been cold and naked."

This is what dying to the world cost Paul. Beatings. Imprisonment. Hunger. Nakedness. Suffering.

And Paul's response? *"I consider them garbage, that I may gain Christ."* Paul didn't just accept this suffering; he counted it as NOTHING compared to knowing Jesus.

Think about what Paul is saying. He's not saying "it was worth it." He's not saying "the reward outweighed the cost." He's saying the cost was GARBAGE. Trash. Nothing. Not even worth counting. The suffering doesn't even register on the scale when you weigh it against gaining Christ. This is what happens when you truly see what you're trading for, everything the world values becomes worthless compared to knowing God.

The Disciples: Leaving Everything Behind

When Jesus called the first disciples, Matthew 4:20-22 says:

"At once they left their nets and followed him... Immediately they left the boat and their father and followed him."

Immediately. At once. No hesitation. No negotiation. No "let me think about it."
They left their livelihood (the nets, the boat). They left their family (their father). They left their security, their future, everything they knew.
Why? Because Jesus called them.

Later, Peter said to Jesus: "We have left everything to follow you! What then will there be for us?" (Matthew 19:27)

And Jesus replied: "At the renewal of all things, when the Son of Man sits on his throne in his glory, you who have followed me will also sit on twelve thrones, judging the twelve tribes of Israel. And everyone who has left houses or brothers or sisters or father or mother or wife or children or fields for my sake will receive a hundred times as much and will inherit eternal life." (Matthew 19:28-29)

This is the promise: lose everything here, gain everything there.

Eleven of the twelve disciples were martyred for their faith. They didn't just lose their possessions; they lost their lives.
And not one of them recanted. Not one of them said, "I was wrong. Jesus wasn't who He said He was." They all died proclaiming the truth. Why? Because they had seen Him. They had walked with Him. They had watched Him die and rise again. They KNEW what they had. And what they had was worth dying for. Their blood is their testimony: God is real, the kingdom is real, and it's worth everything.

THE TYRANT

The Pattern in Scripture

Look at every single person in Scripture who truly followed God:
Abraham left his home and family to go to a land he didn't know. Moses died in the wilderness, never entering the Promised Land he fought for. Isaiah, according to tradition, was sawn in two. The prophets were mocked, rejected, beaten, killed. John the Baptist was beheaded. Stephen was stoned. James was killed with the sword. Peter was crucified upside down. Paul was beheaded.

Every single one of them LOST by worldly standards. Every single one of them suffered. Every single one of them gave up comfort, security, wealth, status, or life itself.

And every single one of them gained life.

This is the pattern. This is the cost. This is the way.

"Enter through the narrow gate. For wide is the gate and broad is the road that leads to destruction, and many enter through it. But small is the gate and narrow the road that leads to life, and only a few find it." (Matthew 7:13-14)

The Question for You

So now I ask you: What does dying to the world look like for you?

I can't tell you specifically what God is asking you to release. But you know. You will feel the tug, the pull, within your heart guiding you.

Maybe it's your career that compromises your integrity. Maybe it's your house that keeps you enslaved to a mortgage. Maybe it's your retirement account that you're trusting instead of trusting God. Maybe it's your comfortable lifestyle that allows you to ignore the suffering around you. Maybe it's your security that has become your idol.

Whatever it is, you know.

And you have a choice: Will you be like Moses, Zacchaeus, Paul, and the disciples, losing everything to gain eternal life?

Or will you be like the rich young ruler, keeping everything and losing your life?

The Cost and the Promise

I'm not going to lie to you. Dying to the world will cost you everything. It might cost you your career, your house, your savings, your relationships, your reputation, your comfort, your plans, your future as you imagined it.

But here's God's promise, spoken by Jesus himself:

"No one who has left home or brothers or sisters or mother or father or children or fields for me and the gospel will fail to receive a hundred times as much in this present age: homes, brothers, sisters, mothers, children and fields (along with persecutions) and in the age to come eternal life." (Mark 10:29-30)

You lose everything here, you gain a hundred times as much. You die to this world, you gain eternal life. You let go of what you can see; you receive what you cannot see.

Every person in Scripture who died to the world had the chance to go back. The cost was everything they owned, everything they were.

Moses could have returned to Egypt. Zacchaeus could have reclaimed his fortune. Paul could have gone back to his former life. The disciples could have denied Christ and saved themselves.

None of them did. Not one chose the world over what they'd found.

The Final Word

Dying to the world is not a one-time decision. It's a daily death.

THE TYRANT

Every morning you wake up, you choose again. Every time you want to hold back, you choose to give. Every whisper of fear, you choose to trust.

"I die every day, I mean that, brothers and sisters, I die every day." (1 Corinthians 15:31)

Paul died daily. Moses chose daily. The disciples followed daily.

And so must you.

This is not a burden. This is a blessing. Because every time you die to the world, new life comes into the spirit. Every time you release what enslaves you, you become more like Him.

This is the irony of salvation: you have to lose your life to find it.

"Whoever wants to be my disciple must deny themselves and take up their cross and follow me. For whoever wants to save their life will lose it, but whoever loses their life for me will find it. What good will it be for someone to gain the whole world, yet forfeit their soul?" (Matthew 16:24-26)

This is what dying to the world actually looks like. Moses walking away from a palace. Zacchaeus giving away his wealth. Paul counting everything as loss. The disciples leaving their nets to follow Jesus.

Faith in action. Trust lived out. Love over fear.

So I ask you one final time: What will you do?
Will you keep holding on to what you can see, or will you trust God with what you cannot see?

Will you keep serving the tyrant of this world, or will you serve the Father of love?

Will you cling to a life that has an expiration date, or will you lose it to gain eternal life?

The choice is yours. The time is now.

Choose.

CONCLUSION: THE TRUTH YOU NOW CARRY

You cannot unknow what you now know.

The tyrant has been revealed. Satan, who has infected every system, corrupted every institution, enslaved humanity through every structure of this world.

-You have seen John's chains.
-You have seen the mathematics of slavery.
-You have seen the web of greed.
-You have seen the invisible cage of laws.
-You have seen the deception of "freedom."

And now you have seen the only path to true freedom: death to this world, and rebirth to life.

This is not a comfortable message for most people. This is not about getting wealthy or living your best life through easy formulas. This is the cross. This is the cost. This is the truth that will either liberate you or condemn you, depending on what you choose to do with it.

The tyrant wants you to do nothing. He wants you to nod your head, feel momentarily uncomfortable, and then return to your enslavement with renewed vigor, working even harder to maintain the illusion of freedom and life.

But God? God wants you to act. To move. To choose. To fight.

Not against flesh and blood. Not against John's boss. Not against the bank. Not against the government officials. But against the spiritual forces behind them all. Against the contamination. Against the tyrant himself.

"For our struggle is not against flesh and blood, but against the rulers, against the authorities, against the powers of this dark world and against the spiritual forces of evil in the heavenly realms. Therefore put on the full armor of God, so that when the day of evil comes, you may be able to stand your ground, and after you have done everything, to stand." (Ephesians 6:12-13, NIV)

Take a stand. Stand against the fear that paralyzes. Stand against the greed that enslaves. Stand against the pride that blinds. Stand against the hate that destroys. Stand against the lust that consumes.

Stand for love. Stand for the light. Stand for life. Stand for God.

This is the battle. This is your purpose. This is why you were born into this contaminated world. Not to be enslaved by it, but to be refined by it, sharpened by it, made pure through the pressure of it.

The tyrant thought he could use suffering to destroy you. But God uses that same suffering to perfect you.

"Consider it pure joy, my brothers and sisters, whenever you face trials of many kinds, because you know that the testing of your faith produces perseverance. Let perseverance finish its work so that you may be mature and complete, not lacking anything." (James 1:2-4, NIV)

So go. Walk out into the world with eyes now open. See the tyrant's work everywhere. Feel his chains. Recognize his whispers.

And choose differently.

Choose to give when the system says take. Choose to love when the world breeds hate. Choose to trust God when fear wells up from the pit of your stomach. Choose to serve when pride demands you be served. Choose life when everything around you chooses death.

This is not easy. This is not comfortable. This is not the path most will choose.

Remember what Jesus said:

"Enter through the narrow gate. For wide is the gate and broad is the road that leads to destruction, and many enter through it. But small is the gate and narrow the road that leads to life, and only a few find it." (Matthew 7:13-14, NIV)

But What Does That Actually Mean?

So what does choosing life actually look like? What do you do tomorrow morning when the alarm goes off and you have to go back to that job, back to those bills, back to that system?

Because choosing life is not a one-time decision. It's a thousand small decisions, every day, for the rest of your life.

God promises to guide your steps: *"Your word is a lamp for my feet, a light on my path"* (Psalm 119:105). Let me show you what that roadmap looks like.

Tomorrow Morning

Tomorrow morning, before you check your phone, before you start your car, before you enter the tyrant's system again, get on your knees and pray.

Not some religious formula. Not memorized words. Speak from your heart to your Father.

Recognize what you're surrendering: Your life carries something within it, desires, goals, direction, a pull toward certain choices.

This is your will.
Each life has its own will. You can choose to guide your own life with your own will. That's a right, a privilege given to you by your Creator. It is yours to keep and use, or to surrender.

The Father is perfect. His plan is perfect. His will is perfect. So you can choose to let your imperfect will guide you, or you can surrender it to Him and let Him create a miraculous life within you: a clean heart and an eternal spirit.

"Father, I see the chains now. I see how I've served the tyrant. I see how greed has guided my hands and fear has paralyzed my steps. Forgive me. Cleanse me. Guide my steps today. I put my life in Your hands. Let Your will be done."

This is your first act. Daily confession. Daily surrender.

This Week
This week, sit down and actually look at your finances. Not to feel guilty. Not to spiral into despair. But to see clearly where the tyrant has his hooks in you.

Calculate how much you actually owe versus how much you actually need.

Ask yourself: "What am I holding onto that's holding onto me?"

Is it the car payment? The bigger house? The lifestyle you're maintaining to impress people who don't care about you? The accumulation that brings momentary pleasure but no lasting joy, and costs you your very life?

Identify one chain. Just one. And begin the process of breaking it.

THE TYRANT

Maybe it's canceling that subscription you don't use but keep paying for. Maybe it's selling something you bought to fill a void that only God can fill. Maybe it's choosing not to upgrade this year when the world screams that you need the latest model.

Small steps. But real steps. Concrete actions. Because the tyrant loses power, the moment you stop feeding him voluntarily.

This Month

This month, practice giving when it hurts.

Not the easy giving. Not the leftovers. Not the comfortable donation that costs you nothing. Not the $5 you forgot you had in your jacket pocket, that's not giving, that's discarding.

No sacrifice means no chains broken.

Give something that makes you uncomfortable. Something that requires trust in God instead of trust in your bank account.

Maybe it's $20 when you only have $50 left until payday. Maybe it's your time when you're already exhausted. Maybe it's extending forgiveness to someone who hurt you. Maybe it's showing love to someone.

Why? Because giving breaks the grip of greed. Every time you give instead of take, every time you release instead of clutch, every time you trust God instead of hoarding, you're choosing life over death.

Remember what He said:

"Do not store up for yourselves treasures on earth, where moths and vermin destroy, and where thieves break in and steal. But store up for yourselves treasures in heaven... For where your treasure is, there your heart will be also." (Matthew 6:19-21, NIV)

This Year

This year, evaluate your enslavement honestly before God.

- Is your job destroying your life?
- Does your lifestyle require you to comply with darkness's demands?
- Are you chasing what perishes?

I'm not saying quit your job tomorrow. I'm not saying sell everything recklessly without wisdom. I'm saying: pray, plan, and prepare to walk away from what enslaves you.

God didn't free Israel in one day. The exodus took time. The preparation took time. But the decision to leave Egypt, that happened in a moment.

What is God calling you to walk away from? Start preparing now.

Ask Him. Listen. Then obey.

I have walked this path. I am currently living it. The fear is real. The uncertainty is real. But God's faithfulness is so overwhelming you cannot imagine it until you're living in it.

His faithfulness is absolute.

The Rest of Your Life

For the rest of your life, remember this truth: you are living in enemy territory.

Every advertisement is a demonic whisper tempting you toward lust. Every bill is a chain wrapped tighter. Every "opportunity" to go deeper into debt is a trap disguised as provision. Every voice telling you that you need more, deserve more, should have more, that's the tyrant speaking.

You must stay vigilant. You must keep choosing. You must keep fighting.

Because the contamination never stops. The pressure never lets up. The tyrant never rests.

But neither does God.

"The Lord himself goes before you and will be with you; he will never leave you nor forsake you. Do not be afraid; do not be discouraged." (Deuteronomy 31:8, NIV)

He walks with you every step. He sees every choice. He knows every struggle. And He is faithful to complete what He started in you.

"Being confident of this, that he who began a good work in you will carry it on to completion until the day of Christ Jesus." (Philippians 1:6, NIV)

A Sober Warning

But I must warn you with complete honesty: if you close this book and do nothing, you are worse off than before you read it.

Because now you know.

Now you've seen.

Now you can't claim ignorance.

"If anyone, then, knows the good they ought to do and doesn't do it, it is sin for them." (James 4:17, NIV)

The question is not whether you'll be judged for your enslavement; we are all enslaved until the Father sets us free. The question is whether you'll be judged as someone who saw the darkness and willingly stayed in it, or as someone who fought with everything in them to break free.

Don't let this be another book you read, nod along with, and then return to your slavery unchanged. Don't let the tyrant use this very book against you, making you feel you did something when you did nothing.

Act.
Today.
Now.
Before you put this book down.

Get on your knees. Confess the contamination you now see. Repent of serving the wrong master. Ask God to show you the first chain to break. Then walk with Him, step by step, day by day, as He prepares you for heaven.

To My Brothers and Sisters,

I want to see you there.

I want to see every single person who reads these words standing in that eternal place, free from the chains that bound us here. I want to see the warehouse worker who gave away his last dollar. I want to see the single mother who chose trust over fear. I want to see the businessman who walked away from wealth to follow the Father. I want to see the young person who rejected the world before it could sink its hooks in deep.

I want to see you, from every walk of life, every background, every struggle, every enslavement. Black, white, brown, rich, poor, educated, unlearned, broken, stained. All of us who saw the tyrant and chose to die to his world. All of us who lost everything here to gain everything there.

I want to sit with you and hear your story. How you fought. How you struggled. How you fell and got back up. How you gave away what you couldn't afford to give. How God provided. How you loved when hate felt safer. How you trusted when fear made more sense. What the Father did for you that you could not have done for yourself.
I want you to see Moses and ask him about walking away from the palace. I want you to meet Zacchaeus and hear how it felt to give away 90% of everything he owned. I want you to sit with Paul and listen to him tell you that every beating, every shipwreck, every moment of suffering was worth it.

Because that's what this comes down to, my dear brothers and sisters. Not theology. Not doctrine. Not arguments about scripture.

This comes down to whether or not I will see you there.

The tyrant wants that seat empty. He wants you to choose comfort now and lose everything forever. He wants you to save your life here and forfeit your spirit. He wants to win. To destroy you.

But I'm fighting for you. God is fighting for you.

Please, choose life.

Not for me. Not even for God, though He deserves it. Choose life because you want to live. Choose life for the spirit that will exist long after this temporary flesh has turned to dust.

Choose life so that when we gather in that place where there are no chains, no greed, no fear, no hate, no suffering, we can embrace as family. As brothers and sisters who fought the same fight. Who faced the same tyrant. Who made the same choice.

What you did before reading this book doesn't matter. The chains you wear don't matter. How deep the contamination is doesn't matter. None of that matters.
What matters is what you choose now, and what you keep choosing at every moment of every day.

"But as for me and my household, we will serve the Lord." (Joshua 24:15, NIV)

I'm not asking you to do anything I haven't done.
I am walking the narrow road. They riddled my car with bullets trying to kill me. I walked away from financial security. I've lost most of my friends to the world. The Father provides for me daily or I do not eat.

This is my choice. I have made it.

And I'm telling you from experience: there is nothing better on earth. I would rather lose everything here and gain life than gain the whole world and lose my soul.

How incredible will it be to have you walking beside me.

The tyrant has been exposed. His power over you is broken the moment you see him for what he is and choose to walk away from his influence.

THE TYRANT

The chains are unlocked. The cage door is open. The path to freedom is clear.

All that remains is your choice.
Will you stay enslaved to death?
Or will you crawl out of the valley of the shadow of death to life?

The tyrant is waiting for your answer.

So is God.

Choose life, my brother. Choose life, my sister.

I'll be watching for you there.

With all the love of the Father,

Justin

THE END

Also by Justin Boynton

- Your Deficiency Beliefs
- Tus Creencias de Deficiencia
- The Final Truth
- La Verdad Final
- The Final Report
- El Informe Final
- Self-Regulation
- Auto-Regulación
- Cries of Justice
- Clamor de Justicia
- The Tyrant
- El Tirano

SOURCES AND REFERENCES
The Car: A Case Study in Systematic Greed
Manufacturing and Component Costs:
Component supplier markup estimates: Industry standard analysis from automotive teardown reports and supply chain studies, 2019-2023.

Assembly labor costs: Bureau of Labor Statistics, "International Comparisons of Hourly Compensation Costs in Manufacturing," 2023.

Shipping and Distribution:
Ocean freight and port fee estimates: Standard automotive logistics industry rates, 2019.

Import tariff rates: U.S. International Trade Commission, "Harmonized Tariff Schedule," Section 8703 (Motor vehicles), 2019.

Dealership Operations:
Dealer markup and fee structures: National Automobile Dealers Association (NADA) data; Automotive News dealership profitability reports, 2019-2024.

Extended warranty and add-on profit margins: Consumer Reports investigations into dealership finance practices, 2020-2023.

Financing:
Auto loan interest rate data: Federal Reserve, "Consumer Credit - G.19," historical auto loan rates, 2022.

Fractional reserve banking practices: Federal Reserve, "Money and Banking" educational resources.

Insurance:
Average auto insurance costs: Insurance Information Institute, "Facts + Statistics: Auto Insurance," 2023-2024.

Insurance company profit margins: National Association of Insurance Commissioners (NAIC) annual reports; major insurer (State Farm, Geico, Progressive) SEC filings, 2023.

CEO compensation: State Farm executive compensation, public filings, 2023.

Fuel:

Gasoline price breakdown: U.S. Energy Information Administration (EIA), "Gasoline and Diesel Fuel Update," 2024.

Federal and state fuel tax rates: American Petroleum Institute, "State Motor Fuel Taxes," 2024.

Maintenance:

Service cost markup analysis: RepairPal industry cost data; Consumer Reports maintenance cost studies, 2023-2024.

Registration and Fees:

Ohio DMV fee structure: Ohio Bureau of Motor Vehicles, "Title and Registration Fees," 2024.

Ohio sales tax on vehicles: Ohio Department of Taxation, "Sales and Use Tax on Motor Vehicles," 2024.

The Phone: A Case Study in Technology Greed

Manufacturing Costs:

iPhone component costs: TechInsights (formerly IHS Markit) teardown analysis, iPhone 13, 2021.

Assembly labor: Foxconn worker wages and assembly time estimates, industry reports, 2021-2023.

Component Suppliers:

Samsung, TSMC, Sony, etc. component pricing: Tech industry supply chain analysis from semiconductor industry reports, 2021.

Rare Earth Minerals:

Cobalt mining wages and conditions: Amnesty International, "This is What We Die For: Human Rights Abuses in the Democratic Republic of the Congo Power the Global Trade in Cobalt," 2016; updated reports 2020-2023.

Rare earth element supply chain: U.S. Geological Survey, "Mineral Commodity Summaries," 2023.

Carrier (Verizon) Operations:

Family plan pricing: Verizon Wireless published rates, 2024.
Network operating costs: Telecommunications industry cost analysis; carrier SEC filings, 2023.
Tower leasing economics: American Tower Corporation investor presentations and SEC filings, 2023.

Apple Services:
iCloud, Apple Music, App Store pricing: Apple Inc. published rates, 2024.
Apple's actual storage costs: Cloud infrastructure cost analysis from industry sources (AWS, Google Cloud pricing as comparison), 2024.
Artist streaming payments: Apple Music reported per-stream rates, music industry analyses, 2023.
Apple services revenue: Apple Inc. SEC 10-K filing, fiscal year 2023.

Data Mining and Advertising:
Google payment to Apple: U.S. Department of Justice antitrust filings, Google search default agreement, 2023.
User data valuation: eMarketer, "Social Media User Data Value," 2023; various tech industry analyst reports.

App Ecosystem:
Google Maps data collection: Privacy policy disclosures and tech privacy investigations, 2023-2024.
Facebook/Instagram revenue per user: Meta Platforms SEC filings, 2023.
Amazon dynamic pricing: Various consumer investigations and academic studies on algorithmic pricing, 2020-2023.

Laws That Protect Greed: Car Dealership Franchise Laws
General Franchise Law Information:
"All 50 states prohibit direct manufacturer sales": Multiple sources:
Wikipedia, "Direct-to-consumer automobile selling in the United States," accessed December 2025.
Federal Trade Commission, "Economic Effects of State Bans on Direct Manufacturer Sales to Car Buyers," February 2024.

U.S. Department of Justice, Antitrust Division, "Economic Effects of State Bans on Direct Manufacturer Sales to Car Buyers," 2009.

History and Development:

Origins in 1930s: Multiple academic sources on automotive distribution history.

State-by-state adoption: Mercatus Center, George Mason University, "State Franchise Law Carjacks Auto Buyers," James M. Hohman, January 2015.

Economic Impact Studies:

"9% price increase from franchise laws": Mercatus Center study (1972 data analysis), January 2015.

"$2,225 consumer savings estimate": Goldman Sachs analyst Gary Lapidus, cited in Federal Trade Commission report, 2000.

"8.6% cost reduction estimate": Analyst report cited in Wikipedia automotive franchise articles, 2025.

NADA (National Automobile Dealers Association) Lobbying Data:

2024 lobbying spending ($5.49 million): OpenSecrets.org, "National Auto Dealers Assn Profile: Summary," accessed December 2025.

2024 political contributions ($3.22 million): OpenSecrets.org, 2024 cycle data.

1990-2006 cumulative donations ($21.17 million, 69% Republican, 31% Democrat): The Crittenden Automotive Library, citing Center for Responsive Politics data.

2009 lobbying ($3.02 million): SourceWatch, "National Automobile Dealers Association," citing OpenSecrets data.

2015 lobbying ($4 million): OpenSecrets.org, "Car Dealers Summary," historical data.

State-Specific Laws and Tesla Disputes:

State-by-state legal status: Multiple sources:

"1 State Laws on Direct-Sales," comprehensive state law summary document (wispolitics.com), 2021.

Wikipedia, "Tesla US dealership disputes," accessed December 2025.
Wikipedia, "Direct selling of automobiles in the United States," accessed December 2025.

Specific State Actions:
Alabama law: Alabama Code § 8-20-1 et seq.
Louisiana 2017 ban: Louisiana Senate Bill 107, enacted June 2017.
Texas, Virginia, Michigan prohibitions: State franchise law statutes and court rulings, various dates.
Massachusetts Supreme Court ruling (2014): Tesla v. Massachusetts State Automobile Dealers Association.
Delaware Supreme Court ruling (2023): Overturning lower court ban on Tesla sales.

Recent Manufacturer Lawsuits (2025):
Scout Motors lawsuit: National Automobile Dealers Association v. Volkswagen Group and Scout Motors, filed February 3, 2025.
Sony Honda Mobility lawsuit: California New Car Dealers Association v. Sony Honda Mobility and Honda, filed August 2025.
Rivian v. Ohio: Rivian lawsuit against Ohio Bureau of Motor Vehicles, filed August 2025.

Consumer Preference Data:
"More than half of dealership customers would prefer to buy directly from manufacturer": Survey data cited in Wikipedia automotive dealership articles and consumer research studies, 2020-2023.

Tesla's Direct Sales Model:
Tesla city center galleries and online ordering model: Company disclosures and business model descriptions, 2010s-2025.
Elon Musk statements on dealer conflicts of interest: Various Tesla shareholder letters and public statements, 2013-2025.

Academic and Government Analysis:
Rent-seeking characterization: Federal Trade Commission economic analysis; various economics journal articles on automotive franchise laws, 2000-2024.

"Protectionism" and "crony capitalism" descriptions: Economic policy analysis from Mercatus Center and other free-market research institutions.

Other Industry Examples (Brief References)

Insurance Mandates:

State mandatory auto insurance laws: Insurance Information Institute, "Compulsory Auto/Uninsured Motorists," state-by-state requirements, 2024.

Certificate of Need Laws:

35 states with CON laws: National Conference of State Legislatures, "Certificate of Need State Laws," 2024.

Hospital lobby influence: American Hospital Association lobbying data, OpenSecrets.org.

Occupational Licensing:

Licensing requirements by state and occupation: Institute for Justice, "License to Work" reports, various years.

Economic impact studies: Brookings Institution and other economic policy research on occupational licensing, 2015-2024.

Pharmaceutical Patents:

20-year patent terms: U.S. Patent and Trademark Office, pharmaceutical patent regulations.

U.S. vs. international drug pricing: Various studies, including RAND Corporation international prescription drug price comparisons, 2020-2023.

General Lobbying Data:

Industry lobbying expenditures: OpenSecrets.org, comprehensive lobbying database, 2000-2024.

A DAY OF LAWS: COUNTING THE CHAINS

Regulatory Frameworks Cited:

Federal Regulations:

Code of Federal Regulations page count: Government Printing Office, CFR annual editions.

Federal Motor Vehicle Safety Standards (FMVSS): National Highway Traffic Safety Administration (NHTSA), 49 CFR Part 571.

FCC regulations: Federal Communications Commission, Title 47 CFR.

FDA regulations: Food and Drug Administration, Title 21 CFR.

EPA regulations: Environmental Protection Agency, Title 40 CFR.

OSHA regulations: Occupational Safety and Health Administration, 29 CFR.

Building Codes:

International Building Code: International Code Council (ICC), current edition.

International Residential Code: ICC, current edition.

National Electrical Code: National Fire Protection Association (NFPA) 70.

International Plumbing Code: ICC, current edition.

International Mechanical Code: ICC, current edition.

State and Local Regulations:

Ohio Revised Code: Ohio Legislature, official statutes.

Columbus City Code: City of Columbus, Ohio, municipal code.

Franklin County ordinances: Franklin County, Ohio, official regulations.

Product Safety Standards:

Consumer Product Safety Commission standards: CPSC regulations, 16 CFR.

UL (Underwriters Laboratories) certifications: UL standards database.

ASTM International standards: ASTM standards for various products.

Department of Energy efficiency standards: DOE appliance and equipment standards.

Employment Regulations:

Fair Labor Standards Act: U.S. Department of Labor, 29 USC Chapter 8.

Equal Employment Opportunity laws: EEOC regulations and guidance.
Americans with Disabilities Act: ADA regulations, 42 USC Chapter 126.
FMLA, ERISA, and other employment laws: Department of Labor regulations.
Food Safety:
FDA Food Code: FDA model food code.
USDA meat and poultry inspection: USDA Food Safety and Inspection Service regulations.
State and local health codes: Ohio Department of Health, Columbus Public Health regulations.
Traffic and Vehicle Laws:
Ohio traffic laws: Ohio Revised Code, Title 45 (Motor Vehicles).
Manual on Uniform Traffic Control Devices (MUTCD): Federal Highway Administration.
School zone regulations: State and local traffic ordinances.
Fine and Penalty Amounts:
Traffic violation fines: Columbus Municipal Court fee schedules, Ohio court costs.
Building code violation penalties: Columbus Code Enforcement fee schedules.
OSHA violation penalties: OSHA penalty adjustment tables, current year.
Environmental violation penalties: EPA enforcement penalty policies.
General Regulatory Count Methodology:
The 2,475 regulatory touchpoints figure is a conservative estimate based on cataloging all federal, state, and local regulations that touch each aspect of John's day, from product safety standards to traffic laws to employment regulations. This does not include the full text of building codes, tax codes, and other comprehensive regulatory frameworks that would push the total into tens of thousands.

THE MATHEMATICS OF SLAVERY

John's Income and Tax Data:

Federal income tax, Social Security, Medicare calculations: IRS tax tables and FICA rates, 2024.

Ohio state income tax: Ohio Department of Taxation, tax rates and brackets, 2024.

Take-home pay calculations: Based on standard payroll deduction calculations for Ohio resident.

Monthly Expense Data:

All expenses (mortgage, cars, insurance, utilities, food, student loans, daycare, credit cards): Drawn from realistic Columbus, Ohio cost of living data and earlier narrative sections of the book.

Days of work calculations: Based on $6,250 monthly gross income ÷ 21 working days = $297.62 per day.

GENERAL METHODOLOGY NOTE

Financial Calculations: All cost calculations, profit margins, and financial analyses in this book are based on:

Industry-standard markup and profit margin data from trade associations and business publications

Consumer price data from government sources (BLS, EIA, etc.)

Corporate financial disclosures (SEC filings for public companies)

Academic and policy research studies

Investigative journalism and consumer advocacy reports

Where specific proprietary data is unavailable, estimates are based on industry averages and conservative assumptions clearly noted in the text.

Regulatory Counts: Regulatory counts represent good-faith efforts to catalog applicable federal, state, and local regulations. Given the complexity and constant evolution of regulatory frameworks, exact counts may vary. The principle demonstrated—extensive regulation of daily life—is well-documented regardless of precise numerical tallies.

BIBLICAL REFERENCES

All Scripture quotations are cited with book, chapter, verse, and translation used (NLT, NIV, etc.) in the text where they appear.

Primary reference: Ephesians 6:12 (NIV) - "For our struggle is not against flesh and blood, but against the rulers, against the authorities, against the powers of this dark world and against the spiritual forces of evil in the heavenly realms."

DISCLAIMER

The author has made every effort to ensure the accuracy of facts, figures, and citations in this work. All monetary figures, lobbying data, and regulatory information are based on publicly available sources current as of the dates cited. Readers are encouraged to verify current figures independently, as economic data, lobbying expenditures, and regulations change over time.

This book represents the author's analysis and interpretation of systemic economic and spiritual issues. Views expressed are those of the author and are intended to promote critical thinking about economic, legal, and spiritual matters affecting modern life.